The Weather
—Fair, high around 60, low in
s. Chance of precipitation is
cent today and 40 per cent
t. Sunday—Cloudy, high in
s. Temp. range: Today, 61-38;
rday, 54-33. Details on page D4

The Washingto

Year ··· No. 108 © 1974, The Washington Post Co. SATURDAY, MARCH 23, 197

Associated Press

Witness Rose Mary Woods, President Nixon's secretary, is escorted by Capitol Police Inspector Leonard Ballard as she appears before the Senate Watergate committee.

Budget Reform Advances

Senate-Passed Version Goes To Conference

By Spencer Rich
Washington Post Staff Writer

The Senate, intent on recapturing the constitutional power of the purse from the White House, yesterday approved a revolutionary congressional procedure of handling the government's $300 billion annual budget. The vote was 80 to 0.

The bill, which now goes to conference with a similar House measure, is a key element in the lawmakers' drive to reclaim decision-making powers that have passed to the White House through congressional sloth and disorganization.

It would create congressional budget committees to consider all federal spending each year as a whole, fix a target surplus or deficit, clamp a ceiling on total outlays, and divvy up the total among 14 broad categories, such as health and defense, and thus assign priorities.

For lack of such mechanism in its creaky procedures, sponsors said, Congress in practice has yielded real control over most budget decisions to the White House, which has a well staffed, centralized Office of Management and Budget capable of coordinating all parts of the budget into a fiscal whole.

They said the new legislation, which also would create a congressional office of the budget (similar in scope to the General Accounting Office) to provide technical expertise, would give Congress the capability to make budget decisions on its own, rather than relying on the White House.

By June 1 and again in September, Congress is to pass resolutions setting out target spending figures for the government as a whole and for each of the 14 major program categories.

The Appropriations committees would continue to act on the spending bills, within the Budget committees' guidelines. If the total adopted in the September target resolution is exceeded by the total of the individual bills, a cutback to comply with the target would have to be enacted.

The bill also would forbid the President to impound for policy purposes any funds voted by Congress.

The drive to revive the powers of Congress over key elements of national life has already led to passage, over a veto, of legislation curbing the President's power to wage undeclared war unless Congress assents, and passage of a bill requiring Senate confirmation of the OMB director. Also part of the drive are efforts to enact curbs on presidential fund impoundments and on executive withholding of documents from Congress. The present bill is another major effort in the same direction.

Senate Appropriations Committee Chairman John L. McClellan (D-Ark.) said he would vote for the bill "reluctantly" because of extreme doubts that in practice it would work as planned. He called it "so fraught with complexities, so confusing and cumbersome" that it might hinder rather than help the goal of clamping a lid on spending. However, the bill's sponsors were more optimistic.

"The bill will give Congress means to deal in an orderly and comprehensive fashion with our most important deci-

See BUDGET, A8, Col. 3

By Ken Feil—The Washington Post

Russell Train explains Clean Air Act changes sought.

Restriction On Gas Sale

By LaBarbara Bowman and Paul Hodge
Washington Post Staff Writers

D.C. Mayor Walter E. Washington said yesterday that the city's voluntary odd-even plan for gas purchases will end next Friday.

"We are returning to normalcy," the mayor said during a news conference, "so we're taking the wraps off."

The mayor instituted the voluntary system, which originated in Oregon, on Feb. 11, almost simultaneously with Maryland and Virginia jurisdictions. It is an attempt to end the lengthening gas lines which had snaked around every open service station, as motorists reacted to the gas shortage.

The odd-even plans in Maryland and Virginia will continue for the immediate future.

Although the odd-even plan is being suspended in Washington on Friday, the mayor said he was still encouraging gas stations to serve only cars which need at least one-half tank of gas.

In other energy announcements the mayor said:

- Eight gas stations throughout the city will be open Sunday from 10 a.m. to 6 p.m. because of having gasoline allotted to them by the city. The mayor instituted the Sunday opening last Sunday with four stations.
- The number of stations remaining open from 7 to 9 p.m., also made possible by allocations from the city, will be reduced from 20 to 12 because business has fallen off, making some of them unnecessary. Some stations have started staying open later without special allocations of city gas.

The city's increased gas allocation for March of 19.3 million gallons, compared to 18.3 million in February, has made the odd-even plan unnecessary, the mayor said. "The long lines have disappeared and the situation is almost back to normal," he added.

"The prospects for continued improvement appear favorable based on the promise of increased gasoline allocations stemming from the lifting of the oil embargo," the mayor said.

Although he forecast normalcy, Mayor Washington added that he still intends to ask Congress for legislation giving him the right to institute some mandatory controls if the gas situation worsens in the future.

Some of his aides have explained that these standby

See ALLOCATE, A8, Col. 3

U.S. Cuts Oil, Gas Estimates

By George C. Wilson
Washington Post Staff Writer

President Nixon's expressed hopes for American independence in fuel received a setback yesterday when new U.S. Geological Survey figures showed substantially less oil and gas under the sea than the government previously had estimated.

Secretary of the Interior Rogers C. B. Morton told Congress in January that it looked as though 200 billion barrels of oil and 850 trillion cubic feet of natural gas could be obtained by drilling into seabeds off the United States.

But new government figures circulated yesterday said the offshore lode could be as low as 80 billion barrels of oil and 490 trillion cubic feet of gas—even counting that already taken from the sea bottoms.

Several major policy decisions, including President Nixon's order for a 10-fold increase in leasing of off shore tracts to oil companies, were made under the higher estimates.

Thus environmental groups who have opposed accelerated leasing of the Outer Continental Shelf on grounds it is too hurried have been handed a new argument.

The new estimates are contained in a report by the Council on Environmental Quality on offshore oil operations. The same report, which became available yesterday, warns that oil may be spilled on beaches if Mr.

See RESERVES, A12, Col. 4

U.S. Air Force Is 'Stronger' Than Soviets', Chief Claims

By Michael Getler
Washington Post Staff Writer

Air Force Chief of Staff George S. Brown says that the service he heads "overall is a stronger . . . more proficient and professional force" than the Soviet air arm and that combat-experienced leadership is a big factor.

The four-star general's enthusiasm for the capabilities of his service comes at a time when military leaders in other branches, particularly the Navy, are painting grim comparisons between U.S. forces and their Soviet counterparts.

During a wide-ranging interview in his Pentagon office, the Air Force's top officer focused on measures other than hardware as a way to equate rival forces.

Without getting into the pros and cons of Vietnam, the general simply pointed out that "that war lasted a helluva long time."

One result, he said, is that "we don't have anyone in any echelon of command in a responsible position who isn't combat experienced. That means a lot in terms of being used to the equipment, the tactics and the people. They've all been exposed to gunfire."

GEN. GEORGE S. BROWN
. . . 'more professional'

The Soviet Union has stayed out of combat since the end of World War II.

All things considered, the general stated, "our tactical forces are far more proficient than those of the Soviet Union." In contrast to what Brown sees as a Soviet fighter force oriented to defense, he said "our tactical forces are trained and equipped to work offensively" in carrying the battle to an enemy.

The general's assessment of U.S. Air Force superiority extends into the airlift and bomber fields as well.

The Soviets, as is well known, "have no bomber force comparable" to the large 496-plane U.S. fleet of long-range B-52 and FB-111 strategic bombers.

The Russians do, however, have a very large bomber defense network of anti-aircraft guns, missiles and fighters. But, under questioning, Brown acknowledged that U.S. estimates indicate that 70 to 80 per cent of the American planes—assuming they are not destroyed on the ground in a surprise attack — could either get through or go around those defenses, attacking from various points around the huge Soviet land mass.

See BROWN, A7, Col. 1

EPA Asks Delay In Clean-Air Rules

By William Claiborne
Washington Post Staff Writer

The Nixon administration asked Congress yesterday to potpone for up to 10 years clean-air deadlines for some heavily polluted cities, and to authorize the government to order electric utilities to shift from oil to coal burning furnaces.

The administration also proposed delaying for two years implementation of automobile antipollution standards, meaning that anti-smog limits for 1975 model cars would be acceptable for 1976 and 1977 models.

The retreat from the original standards of the 1970 Clean Air Act is needed to balance the nation's environmental and energy needs, according to Russell E. Train, administrator of the Environmental Protection Agency.

Train, who unveiled a package of Clean Air Act amendments he sent to Congress, defended the plan as adding "flexibility" to current environmental standards. But in response to questioning, he said some of the proposals would not have been his personal choice.

In fact, Train said, he could not accept two administration proposals, one of which would revoke the law's requirement that existing clean air not be allowed to deteriorate as low as current minimum protective standards and another that would permit power plants to use anti-pollution equipment part-time when regional air pollution standards are not violated.

Train said he was sending those proposals to Congress as "issues" for debate, but not as legislative recommendations.

See POLLUTE, A12, Col. 1

Long-term better air quality doubted. Page A9.

Ford Renews Warning to Europeans

By John Heffernan
Reuter

A new warning to the European allies on the issue of possible reductions of American troops on the continent came yesterday from Vice President Gerald R. Ford.

He cautioned that there could be a unilateral troop cut by the United States unless the allies cooperated in trying to find a mutual and balanced force reduction with the Soviet Union.

Ford's comments were made in an exclusive interview with Reuter and came in the wake of the disclosure by Secretary of State Henry A. Kissinger that American, British and German experts conferred in Washington this week on East-West troop reductions.

Without giving any details, Kissinger cited the tripartite talks in assuring a press conference Thursday that allied consultations were going on despite strains in the alliance.

Kissinger is scheduled to travel to Moscow next week for talks with the Soviets. Subjects are expected to include the current status of the strategic arms limitation talks, East-West security arrangements and possible agreement on mutual and balanced reduction of forces in Europe.

Kissinger's trip is to prepare the way for a scheduled visit to Moscow by President Nixon this summer.

Ford said he was opposed to any decrease in American troop strength in Europe—a position also stated by Mr. Nixon Tuesday night in Houston—unless it was part of a mutual and balanced force reduction agreement with the Soviet Union. But he noted

See FORD, A5, Col. 1

6% Fuel Surcharge On Air Fares Set

By Jack Egan
Washington Post Staff Writer

The Civil Aeronautics Board, citing a "precipitous rise in jet fuel price per gallon," will allow a 6 per cent increase in domestic plane fares starting April 16.

The surcharge will be reviewed by the board after six months, when the CAB will reexamine fuel prices.

At the same time, the board approved a coast-to-coast discount fare filed by Trans World Airlines. It requires reservations and a $20 deposit 90 days before departure. Discounts from normal coach fare range from 16 to 37 per cent, depending on time of year and day of the week.

The so - called "demand scheduling" fare — virtually the only remaining coast-to-coast discount fare — will be available on flights between major Eastern cities, including Washington, and Los Angeles and San Francisco beginning July 8. American Airlines and United Air Lines, which also

See FARES, A8, Col. 1

U.S. Resumes Soviet Credits

After Attorney General William B. Saxbe ruled that U.S. credits to the Soviet Union are legal, the Export-Import Bank approved $74.9 million in loans to the Soviet Union, Poland, Romania and Yugoslavia.

Details on Page A2

Senate Favors Transport to Funeral

POW Kin May Get Travel Pay

By Ron Shaffer
Washington Post Staff Writer

The U.S. Senate quickly passed a bill yesterday that would authorize the Pentagon to pay travel expenses for relatives attending funerals of American prisoners of war and servicemen once classified as missing in action whose bodies have been recovered in Southeast Asia.

The measure was introduced by Sen. Robert Dole (R-Kan.) yesterday morning and was passed by voice vote of the Senate without the usual process of committee study and hearings. Dole said he was prompted to introduce the bill by a story in Friday's editions of The Washington Post.

The Post reported that Cecile Abbott of Sacramento, Calif., thought it "inequitable" that the government would not pay travel expenses for herself and her 12-year-old son to attend the burial in Arlington Cemetery of her husband, Navy Capt. John Abbott, a POW who died in captivity and whose remains were released earlier this month by Hanoi. He requested that he be buried in Arlington.

She contrasted that with the money the government spent to transport relatives of 556 POWs released 14 months ago to reunions in stateside hospitals, and to bring more than 500 of them to the White House for a presidential reception.

Presidential press secretary Gerald L. Warren said at the White House briefing yesterday that President Nixon had asked the Defense Department "to seek avenues" to assist Mrs. Abbott, and the department said it would do so.

Sen. Dole said he would ask the House leadership to vote on the bill Monday. The House was not in session yesterday.

3 Found Guilty of Tax Fraud

Three principal officers of the Pomponio real estate empire were found guilty in Alexandria yesterday of filing false income tax returns.

Details on Page D1

12 Campaign Reform Bills Killed in Md.

By Karlyn Barker
Washington Post Staff Writer

ANNAPOLIS, March 22—A Maryland House committee killed a dozen campaign reform bills today, effectively ending any possibility this year for legislation restricting campaign contributions.

Instead of tightening election law, the House committee amended a measure of Gov. Marvin Mandel to quadruple the amount of money that contributors can donate to state political candidates.

Currently, contributors may give candidates a maximum of $2,500 in the primary and $2,500 in the general election. The amendment by the House Committee on Constitutional and Administrative Law would permit contributors to donate up to $10,000 in each election.

"Everybody thought the $2,500 limit was unrealistic, but nobody had the guts to do anything about it (before)," the committee chairman, Del. Charles J. Krysiak (D-Baltimore City) said. "I think the committee took a stand."

Reform bills, he said, should be aimed "at the big guys getting the big money, not the little guys running for the House of Delegates."

The measures killed by the committee included bills that would have banned campaign contributions by corporations, required the reporting of campaign loans and placed limits on cash contributions.

Those bills and the measure by Mandel to place a $100 limit on cash contributions were proposed here in the wake of political scandals in

See MARYLAND, A6, Col. 6

Maryland redistricted by court. Page A6.

Huge Flock Roosts Anyhow

Sunset Salvo Greets Birds

By Bill Richards
Washington Post Staff Writer

GRACEHAM, Md., March 22 — For more than two hours tonight, men boomed and blasted away with an arsenal of noisemakers in an effort to rid this tiny Frederick County community of millions of birds.

Victory in tonight's engagement between men and birds—most of them starlings, blackbirds and grackles — apparently went to neither side.

At dusk, when the first aerial firecrackers and propane gas explosions boomed out over the countryside, birds by the thousands that were headed for Edger Emrich's 60-acre pine grove, where they have spent the nights since last fall, wheeled and circled in the air, as if confused.

For a half hour they would not land, but as the sky darkened, clouds of birds cascaded into the grove.

About 8:15 p.m., the noise-making ceased for the night and Dr. Kenneth L. Crawford, chief veterinarian for the Maryland State Health Department and coordinator of the antibird campaign, met with newsmen. His view was that this initial engagement—if not the campaign—was won by the birds.

"We lost tonight," he said, "because of a lack of fire-power in certain areas, but the battle isn't over. We will be back again tomorrow and we know what our problems are."

"Some of our people ran out of ammunition," he said, "and our crow call was a flop."

An hour later, encountering a reporter in a restaurant here, Crawford said he

See BIRDS, A6, Col. 1

By Harry Naltchayan—The Washington Post

The birds of Graceham continue to swarm despite efforts to frighten them away.

THE WASHINGTON POST

THE WASHINGTON POST

Views from the Inside

by

Carol Williams and Irwin Touster

Prentice-Hall, Inc., Englewood Cliffs, New Jersey

Printed in the United States of America J

Prentice-Hall International, Inc., London
Prentice-Hall of Australia, Pty. Ltd., North Sydney
Prentice-Hall of Canada, Ltd., Toronto
Prentice-Hall of India Private Ltd., New Delhi
Prentice-Hall of Japan, Inc., Tokyo

Library of Congress Cataloging in Publication Data
Touster, Irwin, 1921–
    The Washington post: insiders speak out.
    SUMMARY: Discusses the background, duties, problems,
and goals of personnel from various departments of this
large metropolitan newspaper.
    1. The Washington post. [1. The Washington post.
2. Newspapers] I. Williams, Carol, joint author.
II. Title.
PN4899.W31W37   071'.53   74-20725
ISBN 0-13-944405-X

Book design by Dann Jacobus

"The Dropouts" by Howard Post is reprinted with permission of United
Feature Syndicate, Inc., New York.

To Bill, Alexander, and Vanessa
C. W.

To my father Ben Touster
I.T.

TABLE OF CONTENTS

FOREWORD

Our purpose in writing this book is to give the reader a sense of the workings and rhythm of a first-rate newspaper. After spending more than a year working with the people on the *Washington Post*, we are convinced that our choice of newspapers was a wise one.

Even if we had not intended to become involved in the daily rhythm of the paper, we found that our needs had to be subordinated to the requirements of people's jobs. We were never able to interview anyone in the newsroom before ten-thirty; reporters and editors on a morning paper don't begin work until mid-morning. One interview took place at police headquarters between two bank holdups. Another was cancelled because the Arab oil embargo had suddenly been lifted and the reporter had to write a story immediately. Interviews with advertising staff were squeezed in between phone calls and sales conferences. An interview with a printer had to be delayed for six months because of labor disputes at the paper.

We were strangers taken in and made to feel a part of what was happening. Interviews were always open and friendly. The only thing that reporters could not understand was that the book wouldn't be in print with the next day's paper.

The authors would like to thank George Kroloff and

Virginia McSweeney of the *Post* staff for making introductions, arranging interviews, and providing us with photographs and documents. Without them we would still be lost in a maze of offices and desks. We also thank the many staff members—reporters, editors, photographers, production people, and business executives—who gave freely of their time to answer our questions.

We are grateful to Katherine Greene whose generosity in providing lodgings made it possible for us to do the research on the book. Thanks also go to John and Pam Pauker for their hospitality and to Reed Whittemore for making our first contact with the *Post*.

CHAPTER 1

A Hundred Years of Growth

During the 1930s a college girl named Kay Meyer spent her summer vacations working as a reporter on her millionaire father's newspaper. Recalling those days, she now says, "There was a great deal of emphasis on having to *do* something. It never occurred to me that I didn't have to work."

Today as Chairman of the Board of The Washington Post Company and Publisher of the *Washington Post*, Katharine Meyer Graham is one of the most powerful women in the United States. Her company owns a media empire consisting of *Newsweek* magazine, the Bowaters-Mersey paper company, six broadcasting stations, a news service shared with the *Los Angeles Times*, part of the *International Herald-Tribune* and the *Trenton (New Jersey) Times*.

The *Washington Post*, the cornerstone of the empire, has come a long way since it started as a four-page sheet selling for three cents a copy in December 1877. Stilson Hutchins, the St. Louis newspaperman who founded it, was convinced of the rather novel belief that a paper could publish the news without being dull. And the *Post* was a combative, lively, partisan newspaper. Hutchins was a Democrat, and he never stopped insisting to his readers that the 1876 election was a fraud and that Republican President Rutherford B. Hayes had no right to be in the White House.

In those days Washington was a collection of villages strung together by unpaved streets, unlighted on nights when the moon was shining as an economy measure. Reporters got around the city on horse-drawn "hacks," on high front-wheeled bicycles, or on foot. They wrote their stories in longhand with heavy lead pencils and, if extra copies were needed, they traced over their original copy with a stylus through carbon paper onto a sheet of tissue paper. It wasn't until the 1890s that two Remington typewriters appeared in the *Post*'s newsroom.

One of the first reporters on the paper, Henry Litchfield West, recalled those days of the 1880s when he was a cub reporter. In the early part of the day he covered events in Georgetown, three miles from the *Post*'s headquarters. Afternoons he walked downtown and checked in at various government departments for news. Then he turned in early copy, walked home to Georgetown for dinner, and walked back downtown to cover night meetings and police work. After turning in his reports around midnight he walked home through Washington's dark streets. He was paid the stupendous sum of seven dollars a week.

It was as laborious to print the paper as to report the news. Type was set by hand, letter by letter, then locked into chases. During the 1880s Stilson Hutchins became interested in typesetting inventions which enormously speeded up the typesetting process. Eventually he devoted most of his time to these inventions and sold the *Post* in 1889 to Frank Hatton, a former First Assistant Postmaster General, and Beriah Wilkins, a former Republican Representative from Ohio. The *Post* was not the first newspaper to use the new typesetting machines (called linotype because they could set a line of type at a time) but it was in the forefront of this technological revolution.

The *Post* pushed for change in Washington during its first twenty years. In the 1870s Washingtonians drank muddy water from the Potomac River and the swampy flats on the riverbank were breeding grounds for mosquitos. Needless to say, typhoid and malaria outbreaks were frequent. For many years the *Post* campaigned for filtered water and for swamp draining. Eventually a water filtration plant was built and the Potomac mud flats were made into a park.

The *Post* also crusaded for the needy. Whenever there was an unusually severe winter poor people suffered terrible hardship. On several occasions the *Post* organized fund-raising drives to collect money for food and fuel in those days before there was any public relief.

The *Post* claimed to represent the interests of all— "negroes" as well as southerners—although a close reading of the paper would undoubtedly show the interests of the latter more prominently displayed. A Richmond, Virginia, bureau was opened in 1882 and the Sunday edition, especially, carried news and features of interest to southern readers. Circulation spread into Virginia and North Carolina.

During these years the paper also covered many outstanding news events. President Garfield's assassination in 1881 provided months of news. His illness and death and the trial of the assassin were front page stories for most of that year. The same year the paper reported a flood which covered the city under six feet of water from the Washington Monument to the Capitol.

The *Post* itself made news on July 16, 1885, when a fire destroyed its headquarters building. The presses were saved but all the type and the subscription books were burned. The *Evening Star* quickly offered the *Post* its plant and the paper appeared the very next day. After a month of repair work the *Post* moved back to the old building.

During the 1880s and '90s, when there was a craze for

puzzles and contests, the *Post* ran several competitions. Once a prize of $30 was offered to the person who could make the most words from the name of President Cleveland's wife, Frances Folsom Cleveland. Thousands of people entered the contest and the winner came up with 2431 words. Before the 1890 census results were announced, the *Post* offered $100 in gold to the person who came closest to guessing the population of Washington. 310,749 guesses were sent in.

Other highlights of these decades were the composition of the *Washington Post March* by John Philip Sousa in honor of the paper and the creation of the Spanish-American War slogan, "Remember the Maine," in a front-page *Post* cartoon. Among the well-known writers whose work was printed on the *Post*'s pages were Joseph Pulitzer and Theodore Roosevelt, although the sketches of Wyoming ranch life which young Roosevelt submitted were not signed.

Under the ownership of Hatton and Wilkins, the *Post* became an independent, nonpartisan paper, particularly concerned with Washington issues and problems. In 1905 the paper was sold to John R. McLean, the millionaire owner of the *Cincinnati Enquirer*. According to his daughter-in-law Evelyn Walsh McLean, John R. "loved power and nothing was too much trouble when he saw a chance to extend his reach and his control of other men." Under McLean civic responsibility took second place to the exercise of power for its own sake and the *Post* became less concerned about advancing the interests of Washington.

John R. McLean was at least involved in the operation of the paper but, when he died in 1916, the *Post* was left to his playboy son Edward (Ned), who had been indulged by his parents and was much more interested in race horses, fast cars, yachts and drinking than in running a newspaper. These were disastrous years for the *Post*, which ended with McLean in a mental hospital and the *Post* being sold at auction after going bankrupt.

Ned McLean's wife Evalyn wrote wistfully in her autobiography, *Father Struck It Rich*, "I think I still believed, in 1916, that given his father's authority, Ned could make the *Enquirer* and the *Washington Post* pedestals for real power of his own. I wanted him to have the admiration and acclaim that go to greatness. . , . They do not teach as plainly as they should, in any school I ever went to, that these things cannot be bought as swift horses, jewels, furs and lawyers' services are bought."

During the presidential election campaign of 1920 Ned McLean abandoned the Democratic politics of his father and supported the Republican candidate, Senator Warren G. Harding of Ohio. He did not publicly announce his support for Harding in his two papers, but he made it clear that he wanted nothing printed that would hurt the Harding campaign.

The Hardings had played poker regularly with the McLeans before the election. After Harding became President, he spent many leisure hours playing golf at the McLean's country estate. Evalyn McLean hoped that her husband's friendship with the President would be a good influence on him.

But by 1923 Warren G. Harding was dead and the scandals of his administration were beginning to come to light. His Secretary of the Interior Albert Fall was being investigated by the Senate for allegedly taking a bribe to lease federally owned oil reserves without competitive bidding. The Senate investigating committee had learned that someone had given Fall $100,000. Fall asked his friend Ned McLean to testify before the committee that he had given Fall the money and McLean lied to protect his friend. It was only thanks to a staff of high-powered lawyers and the confession of the man who had really given Fall the money that McLean managed to escape a perjury charge.

By 1928 McLean was a hopeless alcoholic, mentally ill and confined to a mental institution. The *Post* was increasingly poorly managed and by 1933 it was reportedly losing $1,000,000 a year. Unable to pay its bills for newsprint, the paper went into receivership and was put up for auction on June 1, 1933. Mrs. McLean had made a last-ditch attempt to buy the paper for her sons, but she was not able to raise the necessary capital, and the paper was sold to Eugene Meyer for $835,000.

Under Meyer's ownership a new era dawned for the *Washington Post*. Eugene Meyer, Jr., was the remarkable son of a remarkable father. Eugene Meyer, Sr., came to California from France alone at the age of 16 and eventually became a banker in San Francisco and New York, representing the French firm, Lazard Freres.

Eugene, Jr., born in 1875, grew up in San Francisco, spent a year studying at the University of California, and then went to Yale, where he received his B.A. at the age of 20. After studying international finance and banking in Europe, he worked for his father's firm in New York for four years before opening his own investment banking house in 1901. Within a few years he was a wealthy man, with a seat on the New York Stock Exchange and directorships of a number of corporations.

During World War I he began a career of government service as a "dollar a year man." When he began working for the War Industries Board in 1917, he dissolved his banking firm. Later he was quoted as saying, "If you want to get ahead in politics, keep out until you have made your pile. That's what I did. Once you have money, everything opens up to you."

Meyer directed a number of government financial agencies in the Harding, Coolidge, and Hoover administrations but resigned from government service in May 1933, after Roosevelt had become President. In June he bought the *Post*.

There were rumors that the paper would become a mouthpiece for the Republican Party but Meyer quickly put them to rest by saying, "It will be my aim to improve the *Post*, and to make it an even better paper than it has been in the past. It will be conducted as an independent paper." Meyer's view was that "the newspaper's duty is to its readers, and to the public at large, and not to the private interests of its owner."

At that time the *Post* was competing with four other Washington dailies. To gain circulation Meyer concentrated on improving his editorial page and adding special columns. By 1941 the *Post*'s circulation had gone up 173 percent and its advertising lineage 111 percent. But the paper was still losing $300,000 a year. The reason seemed to be that there was not room in Washington for two morning newspapers—the *Post* and its competitor the *Times-Herald*.

By the end of World War II Meyer was ready to retire from the active management of the paper and he wanted to turn it over to his son-in-law and daughter Philip and Katharine Meyer Graham. Of Meyer's five children Kay was the only one who was really interested in the newspaper. Instead of going to Europe or the country with the rest of the family during summer vacations she worked on the paper with her father. After she graduated from the University of Chicago in 1938, her father took her to San Francisco and found her a job on the *San Francisco News*. Her beat was the waterfront.

"I was the youngest and silliest girl on the paper," she once said, "but the photographers were kind and got me through."

The following year she came back to Washington to work as an editorial writer at the *Post* and met Philip Graham, a young Harvard Law School graduate who was a clerk for Supreme Court Justice Stanley Reed.

Philip Graham was a tall, thin, energetic, and brilliant young lawyer. Born in South Dakota, he moved to Miami, Florida, as a child, where his father took up farming and politics. After receiving his B.A. from the University of Florida in 1936, Phil Graham went to Harvard Law School and graduated magna cum laude in 1939. After a year clerking for Justice Reed, he went to work for Justice Felix Frankfurter, who was a good friend of Eugene Meyer.

Katharine Meyer and Philip Graham were married in 1940. After their marriage Mrs. Graham continued to work at the *Post* because neither of them had a very large salary and Graham did not want to be dependent on his father-in-law.

Phil Graham's legal career was interrupted by World War II. He enlisted in the Army Air Force as a private, then was commissioned as an officer and served in the Pacific. His wife followed him to Army posts around the country and, when he went overseas, returned to Washington to a lowly job on the complaint desk at the *Post*, no longer a potential career woman.

While Philip Graham was in the Army, Eugene Meyer began hinting that he might want to turn the paper over to his daughter and son-in-law. Graham had been thinking of returning to Florida, practicing law and going into politics, but friends in Washington convinced him that controlling a newspaper was not an insignificant source of political influence. In January

1946, at the age of 31, Graham became assistant publisher of the *Post* and six months later, when the 70-year-old Meyer retired to become the first president of the World Bank, Graham became publisher.

Dealing with the *Post*'s financial problems became more urgent after Graham took over since the paper was still losing money and the Grahams didn't have Meyer's fortune to keep bailing it out. Phil Graham also had ambitions for the paper. He wanted to make it a first-rate liberal journal with its own foreign and national correspondents and its own distinguished columnists. This would require money.

Graham decided that buying broadcasting properties would help to solve the financial problem and the *Post* acquired WTOP radio and WTOP-TV in Washington and WMBR (later WJXT) in Jacksonville, Florida. These purchases did bring in revenue but the problem still remained that there were two morning papers in Washington, competing for readers and advertising space.

Graham and Meyer made their first attempt to buy the *Times-Herald* in 1948 after the death of its flamboyant publisher Cissy Patterson, but they were outbid by Colonel Robert McCormick, right-wing publisher of the *Chicago Tribune*. Finally in 1954 McCormick decided he had had enough of the *Times-Herald* and announced that he was willing to sell. Negotiations took place and the two papers merged.

This was the boost that was needed. Now the *Post* had new advertising, new readers, new staff and new features, including comics, most of which were kept. (The *Post* still runs four pages of funnies every day and a large color section on Sundays.)

The purchase of the *Times-Herald* began a period of great expansion. Daily circulation grew from less than

250,000 in 1953 to 532,806 in 1973; advertising linage increased from 25 million lines in 1953 to nearly 85 million lines in 1973. The *Post* hired its first foreign correspondent in 1946; now there are a dozen overseas bureaus. Graham bought the syndicated columns of Louis Harris, Walter Lippmann, and Joseph Alsop, and put together a world-wide news service in cooperation with the *Los Angeles Times*. Then in 1961 he bought a controlling interest in *Newsweek* magazine, which has also prospered under *Post* ownership.

The post-war years were difficult ones for a newspaper publisher of a liberal persuasion. These were the years of McCarthyism, Eisenhower's Republican presidency, and desegregation of schools and public facilities in Washington, D.C., a southern town.

Phil Graham tried to deal with the problems engendered by these issues with decency and integrity. During the period of Senator Joseph McCarthy's anti-communist hysteria, the *Post* printed editorials strongly criticizing the Senator from Wisconsin and taking a firm libertarian position. In the face of bitter criticism and accusations of being pro-communist, Phil Graham stuck by his editorial board and fought for freedom of the press. By doing so, he put the *Post* in a position of leadership with other newspapers and gained some allies.

On the other hand, he took the risk of offending conservative executives of large corporations and losing advertising. Although he did not agree with many of these people politically, he tried to keep up a dialogue with them through his membership in such organizations as the Advertising Council and other business associations. Because he was an attractive and dynamic man, Graham maintained the friendship and respect of many who did not agree with him.

In the 1950s Graham took stands on desegregation which were strong for the times and which also risked the financial situation of the paper. He supported equal rights legislation and the 1954 Supreme Court decision outlawing segregated schools. He also hired the *Post*'s first black reporter and photographer and brought blacks into other jobs in the newsroom. And in the areas where he did not control hiring, in the craft unions, he tried to persuade union leaders to open up the unions to minorities.

By 1960 Graham was suffering from mental illness which became progressively worse. Finally his depression had become so severe that he was hospitalized. One hot summer weekend, Katharine Graham took her husband from the hospital to their farm in Virginia. There he shot a bullet through his head and died on August 3, 1963.

There was, of course, immediate speculation about what would happen to the *Post*, but Mrs. Graham made it clear at a board of directors' meeting after her husband's death that she had no intention of selling the newspaper or any of its divisions. "This is a family business," she said, "and it will remain so. After all, there is a new generation coming along."

During the years when Philip Graham was running the *Post*, Mrs. Graham had concentrated on bringing up the new generation—Elizabeth, Donald, the heir apparent, William and Stephen—and on taking care of her home and doing volunteer social work. But after her husband died, she resumed her newspaper career—as publisher of the *Washington Post*.

For a while she made no changes but studied the operation, asked questions, consulted people on the staff and friends outside. One of her first and most significant moves was to hire Benjamin C. Bradlee, *Newsweek*'s Washington bureau chief as managing editor of the *Post*. (He was later promoted to executive editor and made a vice president of the newspaper.) When Bradlee took over in 1965, Mrs. Graham gave him complete freedom to hire a first-rate staff and reorganize the paper as he saw fit. He was helped by being able to offer top salaries. The *Post* has one of the highest pay scales—at all levels—of any newspaper in the country.

While Mrs. Graham has inherited a strong newspaper tradition from her father and her husband, she has made the *Washington Post* an even better newspaper under her own leadership. Many people faulted Phil Graham for concentrating on editorials and columnists at the expense of news. Katharine Graham started out as a reporter and she still has a nose for news. By choosing first-rate editors and giving them complete freedom to hire staff and organize the newsroom as they saw fit, she has made the paper a place where excellent reporting and writing could be done.

She confers regularly with Bradlee but does not interfere with his decision-making. However, in periods of crisis she does exercise leadership. In 1971 when the *New York Times* and the *Post* obtained copies of the Pentagon Papers and the *Post*'s lawyers were urging caution, Mrs. Graham made the decision that the *Post* should go ahead and print the story.

She also provided firm and steady leadership during the Watergate period. While her reporters and editors were under fire and their findings about the Nixon White House were being questioned, she backed them to the hilt and was willing to risk the reputation of the paper to find out the truth. The result was vindication: a Pulitzer Prize for the paper, respect and adulation for the determination and steadfastness of the reporters, editors, and the publisher.

Since Watergate Mrs. Graham has received citations and honorary degrees; she has been hailed as the most powerful woman in America. But as a newspaperwoman she may have enjoyed her role during the 1974 Newspaper Guild strike more than any of the adulation or honors. While the reporters and advertising staff were on strike, she wrote a few stories (and received bylines for them) and took classified ads over headphones. (One caller told her she sounded over-qualified, that she either knew a lot about a Mercedes or else she must be Katharine Graham.) She couldn't exactly say that she enjoyed the strike, but it was a time when barriers were broken down and, instead of being isolated in her office, she was once more participating in the daily excitement of putting out the paper.

CHAPTER 2

A-1

*A*t three-fifteen every afternoon Jack Lemmon, the night managing editor, rings a triangle to summon the editors to the daily news conference. On Friday, March 22, 1974, they all file into the conference room at the northeast corner of the fifth floor newsroom.

Managing editor Howard Simons takes his place at the head of the large conference table. Ben Bradlee, the executive editor, is on his right and Jack Lemmon is on his left. Bradlee props his feet on the table and peruses the daily news budget—a mimeographed list of the stories which reporters are working on for tomorrow's paper.

The other editors grab news budgets from the table and sit randomly around the room—at the table, on the windowsill, or on low tables at the end of the room. Some who are there have nothing to report but need to know what is going into the paper, like Bob Keith, the editor of the *Washington Post-Los Angeles Times* news service. After the conference he will send out the news budget to the 350 newspapers which subscribe to the service so that their editors can hold open space for the stories which they want to run. Bill Snead, the assistant managing editor for photography, needs to know what pictures are required for the front page. On the national and Metro desks there are deputies and assistants who attend the conference without reporting.

Simons is a quiet, soft-spoken, former science reporter, a foil to the sharp-tongued, impatient Bradlee. Simons nods to national editor Peter Silberman, young, dark-haired, wearing horn-rimmed glasses. Silberman chews on a cigar stub and speaks with a German accent.

Silberman reads from the news budget. In a column on the left side of the page are words in capital letters, used to designate the stories. A reporter writing a story types the identifying "slug" at the top of each page and the printer who sets it in type puts the slug at the top. A description of the story runs across the center of the page and at the right is the estimated number of inches which the story will take and a blank column where the actual number of inches will be filled in.

Under the slug PRESIDENT, Silberman reads, "Nixon names Leonard Firestone Ambassador to Belgium." Down the list. "SAFETY. McDonnell-Douglas says that the DC-10 which crashed near Paris did not incorporate safety devices."

"I wonder how many people are going to sue McDonnell-Douglas," Simons says.

"CONFERENCE," Silberman reads on. "Economist tells Conference Board Session on Energy that the U.S. economy will have to generate $770 billion in capital investment to meet energy needs to 1985 and a Treasury Department expert agrees."

"Soft," Bradlee growls. "Where's the news?"

"$700 billion isn't news?" Silberman asks.

"No, that's nothing."

Down the list Silberman goes. When he finishes, Simons nods to Lee Lescaze, the foreign editor, a bright young Harvard graduate, Chinese specialist, and former reporter. Lescaze points to assistant foreign editor Steve Klaidman who begins discussing items on the foreign news budget.

"SYRIA," he reads. "Syrians bailed out on tentative approval of lifting oil embargo when they discovered there was U.S. pressure to lift it unconditionally, but they are not making a major . . ."

"News," Bradlee interrupts. "Where's the news?"

Next is Len Downie, deputy Metro editor, with shoulder-length brown hair and wearing plaid bell-bottom slacks.

When he begins to read, "ALLOCATE. The odd-even system of gasoline distribution is being abandoned," there are loud cheers. Everyone is looking forward to having an unlimited supply of gasoline again.

He continues down the list to BIRDS. This story had gone on for months. Millions of birds have taken up residence for the winter in a pine grove near the town of Graceham, Maryland, and have resisted all attempts to dislodge them.

"Today," says Downie, "the word is that they are going to be removed. They've got noisemakers, distress calls, and a whole system that's supposed to get them out of there."

Downie's report is followed by a brief one from Hobart Rowen, the financial editor, a small dark man with an elfin face. "The Deputy Director of the Treasury says that the economy has slumped for the second successive quarter. FARES. The Civil Aeronautics Board is expected to approve an increase in domestic air fares." No one comments.

The meeting ends abruptly as Bradlee stands up and leaves the room. Someone following him out quips, "Be back at four and do better next time."

After Bradlee leaves, Rowen turns to Silberman and says, "I still think it was a good story, the one about the $700 billion."

It is now three forty-five. The second news conference will be held around six fifteen. In the intervening two and a half hours editors will be on the phone to reporters on assignment, asking questions, and sending them back for more information. Some stories will be thrown out, others will have to be edited. Lemmon and his staff will be dummying pages—positioning news stories and deciding on headline size and typeface. Lemmon himself always lays out A-1, the front page of the paper.

At six thirty Lemmon rings the triangle again. This time a smaller group of men files in and they take their places around the table. Lemmon puts mimeographed copies of the A-1 dummy on the table for them to pick up.

Downie and Harry Rosenfeld, the Metro editor, sit at the table. Lee Lescaze tilts his chair against the bookcases at the far end of the room. Silberman sits next to him chewing his cigar and Tom Kendrick, the tall, elegant-looking editor of the Style section, sits silently behind Simons.

The leading story at the top right side of the page is ALLOCATE. The odd-even plan for gasoline purchases is being lifted in the District of Columbia, Downie reports amid cheers.

"Can we go away this weekend?" Bradlee asks.

Simons wants to know whether someone has checked exit routes out of the city to see if travel is up.

"We'll do that," Downie says.

"Next, RESERVES," Simons reads. The story is in the right hand column under ALLOCATE.

"The Council on Environmental Quality issued an 800-page report," Silberman says, "which says we have only half the off-shore oil that the oil companies said we have."

"Has George Wilson [the reporter writing the story] read all 800 pages?" Simons asks.

"I think he's read enough," Silberman replies.

The next story, at the top of the page, columns five

and six, is POLLUTE, also a national desk story. "The Environmental Protection Agency is asking permission to authorize shifts from oil to coal and put off applying clean air and anti-pollution standards and Russell Train [the administrator of the agency] is going along with it."

"Well," says Bradlee, "that's one good story and two bad ones. What else? Rose Mary?"

"That's just a picture of Rose Mary Woods going to testify at the Watergate committee," Lemmon says. The photo of Nixon's secretary is in the top left corner of the page.

"Next?" Bradlee asks.

"BROWN," says Silberman. "The Air Force Chief of Staff says that because of combat experience we are ahead of the Russians. This is a big story. Air Force Chiefs of Staff never give interviews."

"Is this a call for another war?" Simons asks.

"No, quite the contrary," replies Silberman. "He says because we've had a war, we're ahead in troop strength, weapon capacity, and all the rest and we don't need to start a war."

"O.K., that's a good story," Simons concludes.

"Well, what about the birds?" asks Bradlee, looking at the bottom of the page.

Downie laughs. "They've gone out with every damn thing you can imagine—firecrackers, propane gas explosions, crow calls, bird distress calls. The noise was terrible. But they're still there and three crows even came down and sat on the speaker."

Next to BIRDS in column eight is MARYLAND. "The Maryland legislature killed all its campaign reform bills and quadrupled the amount that can be given to campaigns," Downie reports.

"Nice, honest state, Maryland," Bradlee remarks wryly.

Harry Rosenfeld, the Metro editor, breaks in. Stocky, grey-haired, in his mid-forties, Rosenfeld had been foreign editor at the *New York Herald Tribune* and the *Washington Post* until Bradlee turned the Metro section over to him in 1970, with the simultaneous mandate to upgrade it.

"Next is BILL," Rosenfeld says. "The Senate passed a bill authorizing the Pentagon to pay for travel for relatives going to prisoner of war funerals. The day after our story yesterday about the POW widow protesting that she would have to pay her own way to her husband's funeral when the government had paid to send relatives to be with the POWs in military hospitals. The bill went right through the Senate by voice vote."

"That's the power of the press," says Bradlee. "Don't you feel powerful?"

Rosenfeld continues. He is pushing another story for the front page. "We've got a great story," he says. "Phillip Berrigan is out demonstrating at the National Security Agency today. Great comparison with what was going on in the 1960s. He's still there but there are no crowds, no fanfare. You can really measure how things have changed."

"No, no," Bradlee says, pushing away with his hand. "That's not a story. What's happened to his wife anyway? Did she get out of the slam?"

"She got a suspended sentence for shoplifting," Downie says.

"FARES," reads Silberman at the middle of the page in columns two and three. "Domestic air fares are going up 6% on April 16."

"Again?" Simons asks.

"What's it going to cost to fly to New York?" Bradlee wants to know.

"Whatever it is," says Downie, "more people are

going to use the Metroliner."

"The next one is CREDITS," says Silberman. "Saxbe ruled that U.S. credits to the Soviet Union are legal and the Export-Import Bank approved $74.9 million in loans to the Soviet Union, Poland, Romania, and Yugoslavia."

"It's got to come off," says Simons abruptly. "What else have we got?"

"Gerald Ford on a troop cut," Silberman replies, "an interview with Bob Heffernan of Reuters."

"John Heffernan," Rosenfeld says.

"O.K.," concedes Silberman, "John Heffernan. Ford had an exclusive interview with him and said that the U.S. may cut troops in Europe unilaterally unless the Europeans cooperate in trying to help in force reduction with the Soviet Union."

"Replace CREDITS with that," Simons said. "What about the Pomponios?" He was referring to a box near the bottom right of the page. "Have we got a story inside on that?"

"Yes," says Downie. The Pomponios had real estate and construction operations in suburban Virginia and had just been convicted for filing false income tax returns.

"Have we explained what's going on in that case?" asks Simons.

"Of course we did," Rosenfeld explodes jokingly. "Aren't you ashamed to ask that question?"

"Is that all?" Bradlee wants to know.

"It's a good story, Ben." Rosenfeld holds out the Berrigan story to Bradlee. Bradlee slaps at it and leaves the room, the others following.

Today is not a big news day. It might seem that the lifting of restrictions on the sale of gasoline is not worthy of being the number one story, but when the thousands of car owners who had been spending hours in line to buy gasoline all winter pick up their Saturday paper to read the headline, they will be pleased, just as the editors are. It is a "good" story for a change, not one which will shock, enrage, or depress readers.

By six thirty the reporters' side of the newsroom is beginning to empty out. The desks facing toward the front of the room are unoccupied except for a few where stragglers are finishing up late stories.

Now the focus moves across the room to the news desk and the copy desks, which are perpendicular to the reporters' desks. Jack Lemmon, his glasses propped on top of his bald head, sits back at his desk, shoves his glasses down again, and looks at the dummy sheets.

The national, foreign and Metro desks each have their own staff of four or five copy editors. They are seated around clusters of desks, bent over their work—writing headlines and editing copy. Between six and eight o'clock they will edit, read, and write headlines for every story in the news section of the paper. (The sports, Style and financial sections have their own copy desks.)

Lemmon gets up and hands the national slot man (the chief copy editor) the page one dummy sheet with headline typeface indicated. Now the headlines for these stories can be written.

From the newsroom on the fifth floor the copy is moved down to the fourth floor composing room. At one end of the room printers are sitting at linotype machines with clattering keyboards. Others are carrying the trays of lead type to tables at the center of the room where other printers are standing over chases (metal frames the size of a newspaper page) where the blocks of type and engravings are laid in columns according to the page dummies. Some editors have come down from the fifth floor to help the printers interpret the dummies and get the type in the right position. The printers are wearing sports shirts and large aprons while the editors are dressed in coats and ties. Overhead containers holding galley proofs are clanking along a conveyor belt from the composing room to the proofreaders' room. The corrected galleys are sent back to the linotype operators so that they can reset any type.

As the chases are filled, one by one, the printers tighten bolts around the edges to lock the type in. Then they lift a metal flag at the bottom of the chase to indicate that it is ready to go. The chase is then slid onto a wheeled table and carried off to be stereotyped. The stereotypers make a positive image of the type, cuts, and engravings on the page form on a fiber mat which is then pressed into a semi-cylindrical form. From these mats curved metal printing plates are cast and sent down to the press room to be fitted onto the presses.

By ten o'clock Lemmon is ready to take a break for a cup of coffee. He has been at work since one thirty p.m. and he won't leave the newsroom until after midnight when the second edition, the late city edition, comes up from the press room. Now he is waiting for the first edition to come up. It's going to be late tonight. It should be up by ten fifteen but tonight it won't be in until around ten forty-five.

When the papers are rolled through the newsroom on a cart, Lemmon picks one up and looks over page one. The headline for the story on oil and gas estimates is too long. It makes the column look top-heavy. He makes a note to have it rewritten for the next edition.

Pictures of the birds at Graceham, Maryland, by a *Post* photographer have come in and the United Press International photo which was used in the first edition can be replaced. He selects a shot of the swarming birds and chooses a second photo for the inside page where the story is jumped. Bill Richards, the reporter, has rewritten his story for the later editions, reporting on the effort to rout the birds until it was abandoned at dark.

His typed story and the photographs have been sent in from Graceham on a portable machine which, when plugged into a telephone, transmits a copy of the document to a receiving machine in the *Post* newsroom. This technique eliminates many of the mistakes which occur when a reporter phones a story in to a typist, who may misunderstand a word or spell a name incorrectly. Lemmon looks over the story. The headline won't have to be changed.

There are a few new stories on the inside pages which will require making some changes—a Watergate story from the *Los Angeles Times*, an Associated Press story saying that Nixon's brother is retiring from the Marriott Corporation, a story by national desk reporter Dan Morgan saying that the United Auto Workers president is urging Congress to ban automobile imports. The Style section will be revised to make room for a piece on an evening social event—all routine, nothing complicated tonight.

Lemmon checks with Barbara Taylor who lays out the Metro pages: no changes there. Rosenfeld played the Berrigan story very big in his section of the paper—a five-column picture of the excommunicated priest confronting a lieutenant colonel. It covered nearly the whole top half of the page.

Around eleven o'clock a photo transmission of the front page of the *New York Times* arrives. About the same time the *Times* has received the front page of the *Post*. Lemmon glances over the *Times* front page. Nothing major. He doubts whether the *Times* will be interested in following up on any of their stories tonight either. If there were a big story, he would have to call up reporters to check it out and fill in whatever new information they could find for the later editions.

Lemmon has been with the *Post* since 1966, bringing with him many years of experience as an editor and teacher. He began his career as a sports editor on a small paper in northern Illinois, after graduating from the University of Illinois in 1949.

During the course of five years in the Navy in the 1950s, he ended up teaching at the Naval Academy in Annapolis and moonlighting at the copy desk of the *Evening Star*. He left the Navy and worked full-time at the *Star* for nine years, becoming head of the copy desk. Then he went to Ohio State University to teach journalism. When he was offered a job as slot man on the copy desk at the *Post*, he accepted.

Most of his life Lemmon has been a daytime person. At the *Star* he worked from seven a.m. to three p.m. and enjoyed the hours. Getting up early didn't bother him and he liked coming home early and being able to spend time with his wife and children.

Now, as night managing editor, he has adapted to a new schedule. "I like the night work from my own selfish, personal point of view," he says. "You don't have to worry about rush hour traffic. You come in in the middle of the day and go home in the middle of the night. I live pretty far out in Maryland and I come in in twenty-five minutes. During rush hour it takes about an hour and a half.

"But I've got a boy now in junior high and I see him on Sunday and I don't see him again until Saturday, which is unfortunate because that's an age when a boy needs time with his father. So there are some drawbacks. And I don't spend that much time with my wife either."

But he wouldn't have missed these years at the *Post*—seeing the paper grow and improve, being involved in the political stories and the Watergate stories. He is one of the few persons who is in touch with all of the parts of the paper: from news gathering to ordering extra space when there is a heavy news or advertising day, even to selecting a new comic strip every now and then.

Lemmon pushes his glasses up on his head, goes over to the copy desk, and asks the slot man to have someone shorten the headline for the oil and gas estimate story.

CHAPTER 3

Metro

There are more than 120 employees of the Metropolitan department, the largest section in the newsroom. Harry Rosenfeld, assistant managing editor/metropolitan, presides over this domain.

"Metro is charged with delivering the local news to our readership," he explains. "Although the *Washington Post* has an eminent national and international reputation, we are a local newspaper—we sell our copies locally. We sell them in the capital of the United States where the primary industry is government, however, making a somewhat unusual audience, but still a local audience."

Metro has the problem of dealing with three very different areas: northern Virginia, the District of Columbia, and the two counties in Maryland which ring the city of Washington. The city of Washington itself has a predominantly black population. Many of its citizens are middle-class civil servants but many are poor and live in the deteriorating sections of the city. The surrounding counties are made up of an inner ring of older communities and an outer ring of burgeoning suburbs all different from each other. Montgomery County, Maryland, has one of the highest per capita income rates in the country, while neighboring Prince George's County is predominantly populated by people with lower incomes and is beginning to develop some of the health, welfare, and housing problems of the inner city. Alexandria, Virginia, is a city older than Washington itself, while the subdivisions of Prince William County, Virginia, have been bulldozed out of prime farmland in the past five years.

The traditional newspaper practice is to give experienced reporters assignments in the city and send inexperienced ones to the suburbs to learn their trade covering zoning hearings and school board meetings. Rosenfeld did not feel that this traditional practice was adequate. "We decided not to write a lot of little stories about a lot of little places. Instead we have been trying to write and report stories in such a way that a total stranger would be interested. For example, if we were writing about teachers' salaries in the District, we would also show teachers' salaries in all the other communities we serve. And also show what is happening in terms of teachers' salaries—are they going up or down, and what has been done to the quality of teachers. These are things people can understand and it is useful information touching on their own lives."

As a former foreign editor he draws on his experience to train reporters. "I tell my Metro people . . . they should regard it in some ways as a foreign assignment. They should be knowledgeable about everything that happens in that county, gather string all the time and write when they have enough for a real story. That's . . . made possible the assignment of senior reporters to the counties. They don't have to do diddly work any more, they're doing respected work."

Metro has bureaus in each of the Maryland and Virginia counties around Washington as well as the capitals of both states. Most of the District of Columbia reporters work from the *Post* newsroom but some are assigned to police headquarters and the local courthouses and rarely come to the office.

The *Post*'s Fairfax County, Virginia, bureau is across

the Potomac River from Washington, in the town of
Fairfax. The three-person office is a bleak anonymous
room in the county courthouse. There, behind a typewriter, sits Judy Nicol, one of the three reporters
assigned to cover Fairfax County.

A pleasant woman in her early thirties, Judy Nicol
came to the *Post* in 1973 from the *Chicago Sun-Times*
where she was a general assignment reporter, usually
covering the politics of health care delivery. After six
months in Fairfax County she is feeling the frustration
of trying to understand an area which is new to her and
where there are not many handles for learning what is
going on.

She points to a large map on the wall. "There are 405
square miles in this county," she says, "and no center,
no point of congregation, no central shopping area or
political center. There are so many communities that it
is impossible to learn the names of them, much less the
names of the political and civic leaders.

"Look," she says, "here's a directory of civic associations. There are about 400 organizations listed in
there—everything from block clubs to large groups."

In Fairfax County there is not much automatic,
breaking news, like fires, police action, strikes. There is
very little poverty or racial tension; social or economic
conflicts are rare. Population statistics show that the
median age is high and the birth rate is very low.
Fairfax County is an area of older people with relatively
high incomes. They are concerned about land development and sewer hookups and to a lesser degree about
education and the quality of the environment.

"It's really a feeling you're trying to discern," Nicol
says. "Harry Rosenfeld asks for stories about what
people do, what is it like to live in Fairfax County, a
slice of life. But to make the stories meaningful you

have to have a sense that it's a true slice of life you're writing about."

In January 1974 before the gasoline shortage had reached its peak, Nicol went through the census reports and chose a tract in the community of Annandale which came close to having the average income, age, type of housing, number of children, and other statistics for the county. Then she went from door to door asking people what they thought about the impending energy crisis. Was it real? How would it affect them? What would they do about going to work, shopping, getting around, in an area where public transportation is inadequate?

The main problem she encountered was that people weren't home, even late in the afternoon. But she found that the people who were home were lonely and eager to talk, not just about the energy crisis but about their lives. One man told her about how his wife died of cancer; a woman had a long conversation about how her daughter's husband had left her and how terrible this was.

Nicol interviewed 30 people in four days and felt that the experience was rewarding. "It really gave me a sense of what people thought. Sometimes I spent an hour to an hour and a half with a person just standing and talking through the screen door."

She is prepared to do this kind of interviewing again, or to drive around to the various communities, introduce herself, and talk to presidents of the local chambers of commerce to find out what is going on.

Washington is very different from Chicago, she finds. Chicago is a city of action—crime, tragedies, scandals, political deals, and conventions. The city desk handles all local news. In Washington, since the federal government is the city's biggest business, the national desk covers all the big Washington stories which have national impact, while Metro covers only local stories. Watergate, of course, was the great exception. It began as a local story because the break-in at the Democratic Party headquarters was a police story. As the story became bigger, Harry Rosenfeld had to fight to keep it on the Metro desk.

The *Post* and the *Sun-Times* differ also. At the *Sun-Times* there was more news and there were fewer reporters than at the *Post*. The *Post* is more selective about what it covers. Because of its large staff, it can assign a reporter to work on a long investigative series for several months. A paper with a smaller staff has to keep its reporters turning out copy every day to fill up the pages. Reporters at the *Post* are also more competitive with each other than they are at the *Sun-Times*. Sources are shared reluctantly, and story assignments often arouse jealousy.

Judy Nicol came to Washington because her husband, also a journalist, got a job on another Washington paper. She applied for a job by letter from Chicago and received no reply. Finally she phoned to ask if the letter had been received and was told it had been. Then she phoned again, said she was going to be in Washington, and asked for an interview. She was first interviewed by Elsie Carper, a veteran reporter, now assistant managing editor for personnel. Then she talked to Harry Rosenfeld, Barry Sussman (the District of Columbia editor), Howard Simons, and Ben Bradlee. A few days after the battery of interviews, she was told that if her references checked out she would have a job. About a week after that she was asked to report to the newsroom in two weeks.

For three months she was assigned to the District of Columbia doing general assignment work. Then she worked on some minor parts of the story of Vice President Agnew's resignation before being assigned to Fairfax County.

Many reporters would prefer to work in the city because the suburban assignments are far from where they live, they have to attend night meetings, and they have contact with editors and other reporters in the newsroom only by phone. They also have to file their stories by telecopier and never get a chance to be beside the editor's desk while the story is being read to argue the merits of this phrase or that word.

Judy Nicol lives in Montgomery County, Maryland, on the other side of Washington from Fairfax County, about 30 miles away. She puts in long days Monday through Friday, from around ten o'clock in the morning until around eight at night, sometimes later. Her husband is able to go to work earlier and get home earlier, in time to cook dinner for their ten-year-old daughter. "I hardly get a chance to see her except on weekends," Judy Nicol says regretfully.

She has wanted to be a reporter for as long as she can remember. She grew up on a farm in rural Michigan and went to college at Michigan State where she majored in journalism and worked on the *Jackson Citizen-Patriot*. Then she got a job on a suburban Chicago paper where she worked for two years. After nine months at the *Chicago American* she went to the *Sun-Times* in 1969.

Nicol came to the *Post* as an experienced reporter, which is the traditional pattern, since the *Post* does not usually hire anyone who has worked for fewer than three years on another paper. Since its salaries are among the highest in the newspaper business ($450 a week for experienced reporters), and its working conditions and reputation are good, people do not want to leave and the editors can afford to be selective in their hiring.

The *Post* does have an intern program, however, to train talented young people and groom them as possible *Post* reporters. There is a summer intern program for college students and a two-year program for minorities in the news business, that is, blacks, Spanish-speaking people, and women.* There is tremendous interest in both these programs and the competition to get in is fierce. In 1973, for example, there were over 1500 applications for the 18 summer internships.

One person who made it into the two-year internship program is Laura Kiernan, a lively and sharp young, hard-working reporter. She attributes her good fortune to "just being in the right place at the right time" but her story suggests that there is more to it than luck.

When Laura Kiernan was editor of the weekly college newspaper at Catholic University in Washington she also worked as a stringer for the *Post*; that is, she submitted articles to the paper on campus affairs and was paid by the article.

She had applied for a summer internship at the *Post* in 1971 and was turned down. When she graduated in 1972 she applied to the *Post* again, this time as a copy aide or news aide. These are young people who help out

---

* The *Post* is making a bona fide effort to find talented staff people from minority groups. There are, however, many more minority group members among junior reporters than there are at senior levels. For example, at the front page news conference one woman was present and no other minority people attended. At the Metro news conference there was one woman and only one black. One of the complaints of staff members and readers from minority groups is that the decisions about what goes into the paper are made by white male editors and that their viewpoints are ignored or distorted.

in the newsroom with the most routine jobs—sorting mail, running errands, answering the telephone, and compiling short news items and announcements. There was no answer from the *Post*, nor from the dozens of other places where she applied for writing jobs, so she settled for a job as a waitress. "I lasted four days," she said.

Finally one day in late June, Kiernan was walking downtown and found herself near the *Post* building. "So," she said, "I just went up to personnel and applied again for a job as a copy aide or news aide. I had to convince the interviewer that I wasn't trying to move up, that I just wanted to stay a copy aide or news aide. I don't think he believed me but anyway two weeks later Paul McCarthy, who is in charge of copy aides, called me up for an interview and I got a job."

As a copy aide Laura Kiernan learned how to make herself useful. She started out working part-time during the week and compiling short items on criminal apprehensions and convictions on weekends. She knew the religion editor, who was short-staffed, so she filled in there from time to time.

One Saturday morning she came to the attention of Harry Rosenfeld when he heard her handling a screwball telephone call with tact and diplomacy; he told her he liked the way she answered the phone.

In August, about a month after Kiernan had started working, the news aide who compiled crime and justice items full-time resigned and suggested that Kiernan ask for her job. Kiernan made a list of all the calendars of events as well as the crime and justice items and told Harry Rosenfeld that she would be willing to do all of them.

"So," she said, "then I had a desk and a typewriter and a phone. All the time I was looking for places to write. Panorama, the Thursday suburban roundup, was a good place to start. The editor is nice and he's willing to give you a break.

"Then I arranged to put suburban jurisdictions into the crime and justice section; so I drove around to all the suburban communities to get to know the cops so I could call them every day for information. That's how I got to work on the big Arlington bank robbery where the guy also hijacked a plane to get away. I had made a routine call to the police one morning and they gave me the story. A lot of other people were assigned to it too, of course."

In January Laura Kiernan applied for a two-year internship, and was accepted. Now as a "floater" on the Virginia desk, she covers stories that fall between Arlington and Alexandria, including the Washington National Airport, and takes assignments that neither of the full-fledged reporters assigned to those desks has time to cover. She wrote a front-page story originating from the airport about a Congressman who was alleged to have beaten up an airport policeman who stopped him for a traffic violation.

She also covered a grisly rape-murder case which was in the headlines for weeks. "That story really drained me," she said. "It was a terrible strain." She interviewed the victim's father and the whole family of the offender as well as doing a general piece on sex offenders.

But she's also done human interest stories like the touching case of a baby with cystic fibrosis who was adopted by her doctor when her parents, who had already lost one baby to the disease, said that they could not keep her. "That one got on the Walter Cronkite show," Kiernan said proudly.

She considers herself lucky but she has also worked very hard to achieve what she has and she has looked for ways to make herself useful, little "ins" where she can prove herself and be noticed, which is important. In the large newsroom where 60 Metro reporters are competing for front-page stories she has to work hard to make a place for herself.

Laura Kiernan's husband James Rowe is also a *Post* reporter, with the financial section. They are both immersed in their work and many of their friends are journalists too; at parties the conversation inevitably turns to stories people have written. "And that is sometimes a problem," she acknowledges. "I do stories that people like to talk about. Like the rape case. I've retold that story so many times at parties that my husband is literally bored to death by it, and finally I didn't want to talk about it any more either."

The news aide who has taken over many of Kiernan's old assignments is Frank Jones, a young man who started out at the *Post* in 1970 as a copy aide. Copy aides do the most routine work and some eventually work up to news aide. One news aide writes the daily weather report, another runs errands for the news desk at night, and Frank Jones puts together calendars of events.

Every day he assembles the crime and justice section by taking items off the District of Columbia police teletype and calling the public information officers of the various Maryland and Virginia police departments. He also writes a weekly calendar of events in the District of Columbia which appears every Monday, a calendar of church events which appears every Saturday, and a weekly roundup of the votes of area Congressmen which is put into Sunday's paper.

Writing these calendars is an exercise in news judgment. Jones has to sift through dozens of items which are sent in, decide which ones are the most interesting to the general public, and rewrite them in a uniform style. Every Monday he has to answer dozens of phone calls from people who want to know why their item was not included in the community calendar.

In addition to doing these regular tasks, he occasionally writes two- to three-paragraph stories and obituaries. These require a lot of rewriting and a great deal of diplomacy in dealing with the relatives of the deceased person. When a written obituary is sent in, it usually contains three or four pages of adulation and very few facts, so it has to be completely rewritten. When someone phones or comes in with an obituary, Jones has to try to ascertain the cause of death and basic information about the person without offending anyone. This is often difficult because relatives frequently do not want to say that the person died of cancer, for example, or they want to hide the fact that the person committed suicide.

Frank Jones would like to become a reporter eventually. He has a year and a half of college to finish before he receives his B.A. in English and hopes to go to school part-time while he is working. Meanwhile, he is earning a good salary and feels that he has been gaining useful experience. News aides, although among the lowest paid *Post* employees, earn over $200 a week after four years.

One of the traditional sources of big city news is the police department, with round-the-clock breaking stories on burglaries, bank robberies, automobile accidents, murders, and rapes. At the *Post* the night police beat is the traditional slot for breaking in young reporters, and for many generations they have either made it or failed on the basis of whether they could survive those first few months of phoning in accident reports from the police department news room at two o'clock in the morning.

Night police is a testing ground but day police for over 40 years has been the province of Alfred E. Lewis, who is something of a legend in Washington newspaper circles. A short florid man with curly grey hair and expansive gestures, he often wears a navy blue regulation police sweater and probably knows more about what goes on in the District of Columbia police headquarters than anyone else in the building. He is friendly with everyone from the deputy police chief to the elevator operator and can tell you when a secretary is going to retire or when an official's last child was born.

He has been at police headquarters so long that his colleagues suspect that he is more cop than reporter. "But it's not true," he protests. "I keep them on their toes. Why just the other day I filed a story on a cop who was charged with drunk driving and suspended."

Al Lewis is also legendary because he never writes a story. He always phones in the information to someone on the desk and his stories usually appear with a double byline. He is a veteran of the days when there was always a rewrite man on the city desk and reporters often phoned in the information for their stories when they were in a hurry.

Al has a sharp memory for detail and for names. In 1935 Eugene Meyer had just hired Ray Clapper, a former United Press International Washington bureau chief, as national editor. Lewis was at that time a copy boy for the *New York Graphic* and had run errands for Clapper on his trips to New York. The young copy boy had taken a vacation and come to Washington to see the sights. His first night in the city he wandered into the old *Post* building at 14th and E Streets and met Clapper coming down the stairs.

"Hey," Clapper said, "I know you want to be a

reporter. I'll get you a job."

Lewis protested but Clapper hustled him upstairs to the city editor Luther Huston who said, "What I need is a copy boy to get the paper out tonight."

So Al Lewis was hired on the spot at $12.50 a week and never went back to New York. Two weeks later he was a reporter, his salary was raised to $14.50, and he has been at police headquarters ever since.

For the first nine years he worked at night and he liked the atmosphere on the night beat. "Night people have camaraderie; there is an atmosphere of friendliness and trust. The day people are competitive and ready to stab you in the back."

For years Al Lewis and Harry Gabbitt, the police reporter for the *Times-Herald*, worked together. Gabbitt would bring in nice bag lunches that his wife had made, go out for some beer, and give the lunches to Lewis. Then when Gabbitt got drunk, Lewis would phone in his stories. After the *Post* and the *Times-Herald* merged, Gabbitt came over to the *Post* as night rewrite man and wrote many of Lewis's stories.

In the 1930s and '40s murders and holdups were big news. The National Theater was just down the street from the *Post* and an eight thirty edition featuring the latest crime was peddled on the street for the theater crowd. Nowadays there is more interest in crime trends —are narcotic arrests up or down? Are there more drunken driving arrests than there were this time last year? "For example," Lewis says, "there were two bank robberies the other day that didn't even get into the paper."

In all his years of reporting the biggest story he ever worked on was Watergate. "I broke that story," he says proudly. On Saturday, June 17, 1972, Lewis was ready to go out to lunch with friends when he got a call from an editor about a break-in at the Democratic National Committee headquarters. Lewis went down to the Second District police station to check out the story. When he reached the police station he met acting police chief Charles Wright, whom he knew well, and they rode over to the Watergate building together. TV cameramen and reporters were clustered around the front of the building but Wright led Lewis to the back entrance and they rode up to the offices on the freight elevator.

"I never left that building for 48 hours," Lewis says. "I phoned in all the information and even sent a diagram of the office. I knew something political was involved because of the bugging devices and the faked names and the money that was found on the guys."

On the basis of Lewis's information Carl Bernstein and Bob Woodward began the investigation that led to all the Watergate revelations.

Al Lewis has been at home in the Police Department press room for nearly 40 years. Every day he comes in around ten thirty in the morning after checking in at the *Post* newsroom for mail and messages. He hangs his porkpie hat and raincoat on a hook on the wall, opens his locker which is filled with a thirty-year accumulation of clutter, gets out his blue police sweater and puts in his brown bag lunch. Every day his wife packs him a sandwich and a piece of fruit. He prefers her food to restaurant fare since he is on a salt-free diet for high blood pressure.

"That's what this business does to you," he tells a visitor, "high blood pressure, an ulcer, headaches. I'd really like to be out on the golf course today to get away from it all."

Lewis sits down at his grey metal desk. A tiny, blonde young woman in a miniskirt swings in and sits at one of

the other metal desks. "Hi, Uncle Al," she says cheer-
fully.

"Hi, Toni, what's new?"

"A police inspector was shot over in Northeast. I'm
just checking it out." She talks on the telephone for a
few minutes and hangs up. "It's nothing," she says, "just
a couple of kids with a beebee gun." She leaves the
room again.

"That's Toni House," Lewis explains, "the police
reporter for the *Star*. Young enough to be my daughter,
but I can't forget that she's my competition. And she's
quick too. She never stops moving."

He gets up and prepares to make his rounds. He has a
few cases to check on—a murder suspect who has been
extradited and is being flown back to Washington
today, a hearing before a judge on a suspected arson
case, and of course a lot of new cases that will come up
during the day. It will be seven or eight o'clock before
he will be able to take the bus home to Silver Spring,
Maryland, where his wife will have dinner waiting for
him. Beef stew tonight, she had told him before he left
that morning.

As the day wears on, the Metro news budget is
shaping up. Al Lewis has phoned in to the District of
Columbia assignment editor; Tom Wilkinson, the Virginia editor, has heard from Judy Nicol, Laura Kiernan,
and his other reporters. He has a good idea of how the
news is shaping up. Herb Denton on the Maryland desk
has one reporter working on a political corruption story
and another has just phoned in to say that Spiro Agnew
sold his house for $350,000, $110,000 more than he paid
for it.

At four forty-five on Wednesday, March 27, 1974, the
Metro editors sit in the conference room to discuss page
B-1. Harry Rosenfeld is at the head of the table with

Len Downie on his right and Barbara Taylor, the news desk editor who lays out the Metro pages, on his left. Rosenfeld runs down the list—area unemployment declines after the energy crisis, independent gas stations are staying open at night now to sell more gasoline. Barbara Taylor points out that the photo which is supposed to go with that story shows an Exxon subsidiary, not an independent, so a photographer will have to be sent out to take another picture.

Next is a story saying that D.C. mayor Walter Washington has announced that he may run in the 1974 mayoral election. "That should be A-1," Rosenfeld says. "If it's not it's unbloody fair."

On Thursday morning the Walter Washington story ends up in the middle of B-1. The lead story on the right side of the page is the lowered unemployment rate in the wake of the energy crisis. The independent gas story is right in the middle of the page with a photo of a Scot gas station right at the top. Spiro Agnew's house sale is at the bottom.

Neither Laura Kiernan nor Judy Nicol has a signed story in the paper. Kiernan had been covering the Alexandria bureau while Joanne Omang, the regular reporter, attended the trial of the Pomponio real estate operators. Nothing came up to write about. Nicol covered a zoning board meeting but nothing happened that was worth a story. Al Lewis phoned in several times during the day, about two Washington banks that were robbed, a stabbing, and a policeman who was freed of perjury charges in an inquiry on police corruption. Nothing appeared about the stabbing; the bank robberies were written up with another robbery of a bank in Virginia and the perjury story appeared as a short unsigned item in a page of news briefs. Frank Jones wrote a three-paragraph obituary of an 87-year-old woman.

CHAPTER 4

The White House and the Hill

Washington's main industry is politics. Mealtime conversations, coffee break gossip, and livelihoods revolve around who is in office and what legislation is before Congress. Naturally the federal government is the primary interest of the press in Washington. All the major papers in the country have at least one Washington correspondent and the *Post*, of course, has many reporters covering different agencies in the federal government—the Supreme Court, the State Department, the Justice Department, the various regulatory agencies.

The most visible symbols of the power of the federal government are the White House and the Capitol, on Capitol Hill (not really much of a slope, but known to Washingtonians as "the Hill"). One of the *Post*'s White House reporters is Carroll Kilpatrick, a soft-voiced, silver-haired Southerner, who has covered three presidents—Kennedy, Johnson, and Nixon. When asked to describe his day at the White House, he laughs, a bit ironically.

"Well, you spend a good deal of time there. The mornings are taken up pretty much with briefings. The briefing with the press secretary is supposed to be at eleven. We frequently have another one with somebody else. This morning we had two others, one with the Secretary of Transportation on the transportation bill and then we had one later with Dr. Tkatch because the President had his physical today. So the mornings are pretty busy and it's hard to get out of there. I mean it's hard to wander around. You have to be there for those things. And then I try to see people for lunch. I try to see other people in the afternoon. One or two or three people in the afternoon, in the Executive Office Building or elsewhere in the government. Sometimes I go up to the Hill to talk to people who have been there. It's just that type of talking to as many people as I can, on the staff and elsewhere."

The fascination of covering the White House is, of course, the chance to be close to power, to get big stories—major announcements, international summit meetings, presidential political campaigns. There is more to reporting the White House than quoting from a transcript of a press conference. It is not just the facts that are important.

Edward T. Folliard, who covered the White House for the *Post* from Calvin Coolidge to John Kennedy and who is now retired, put it this way: "Reporters go to a White House news conference not simply to hear the President announce important actions; after all, such announcements could be made by a press secretary or some other official. They like to know something about the President's mood, his aims and hopes and fears. As the eyes and ears of the American people, the reporters think this is important."

And this is what Kilpatrick was trying to convey in a story written from Houston, Texas, on March 19, 1974, when President Nixon spoke before the National Association of Broadcasters: "Although he appeared somewhat less assured than he did last Friday in Chicago and more tense than in the relaxed setting of the Grand Ole Opry in Nashville Saturday, the President seemed to make a hit with his audience . . ."

But in between the big events "there are long periods

43

of famine at the White House," as Kilpatrick puts it, "where there isn't any great development happening and where the President is not making news, where he doesn't want to talk because he's making plans or what have you." He recalls that the veteran White House reporter Folliard once said, "Covering the White House is feast or famine. You either work eighteen hours a day or you don't work at all."

On the slow days the reporters sit in the White House press room waiting for something to happen. Or they try to talk to members of the President's staff, often without success. Or they make appointments with members of Congress who have talked to the President. The briefings are often routine and do not contain any information that can be used in a news story but, as Kilpatrick puts it, "they're absolutely essential for covering the White House. At the briefings you get the announcements, you get the schedule, you get the planning. That's just routine but you have to know that to know where to go from there."

So the White House reporters are, in a sense, prisoners of the White House. They are dependent on the President for information and he has the power to cut them off totally from sources of information if he so desires. And he often does. As the Watergate crisis deepened, President Nixon, never a gregarious person, became even more remote; he did not see many members of his staff, so very few of them knew what he was thinking.

Lyndon Johnson, on the other hand, loved to talk and wanted people around him, but he wanted to manage the press. He once said to a group of reporters on a flight from the LBJ Ranch to Washington: "If you play along with me, I'll play along with you. I'll make big men of you. If you want to play it the other way, I know how to play it both ways, too, and I know how to cut off the flow of news except in handouts."

President Kennedy was not intimate with reporters as Johnson was, except for a few personal friends like Ben Bradlee, who was then the *Newsweek* Washington bureau chief, but he was fair. Reporters could ask for information and get it. As Kilpatrick recalls: "It was possible to go to Salinger or Sorenson or Ted Clifton or somebody like that and say, 'Look, what does the President mean by this? What's he trying to do?' and they'd say, 'Well, I'll ask him,' and either they'd run into his office and come back and tell you or they would say, 'Come back tomorrow. I'll see him tonight and I'll tell you in the morning.' And sometimes they'd say, 'He says he doesn't want to talk about it.' Or sometimes he'd say, 'Well, tell him one, two, three,' and you'd have a good story because you knew it came straight from him."

Kennedy was a favorite with reporters. He was witty and quick and very good at press conferences. There was little friction between him and the reporters who covered him, although he had his favorites who received special treatment.

Since then the relationship between the press and the President has deteriorated. "Both Nixon and Johnson had a really strong temper and they disliked the press very intensely," Kilpatrick says.

Lyndon Johnson was unpredictable and emotional in his relationship with the White House press corps. For weeks at a time he would refuse to see anyone and not allow his press secretary to give out any information. Then he would suddenly do an about-face and invite a group of reporters to the LBJ Ranch or have them in for a drink at the White House and talk for hours.

The element of surprise and unpredictability made

life difficult for everyone in Lyndon Johnson's orbit. For example, he seldom announced his schedule in advance. Not even his wife knew what he was going to do next. Kilpatrick recalls sitting in the office of press secretary George Christian one day when the phone rang. Christian answered it and said, "Yes, ma'am. No, we don't know what he's going to do tomorrow. We don't know whether he's going to Texas. If he decides to go, we'll let you know and you'll be the first one we'll call." Mrs. Johnson had to keep her bag packed, as did the reporters.

LBJ seldom announced press conferences in advance either. "I could never go to lunch," Kilpatrick recalls, "without thinking he would have a press conference while we were at lunch." Johnson's unpredictability also made Kilpatrick's life difficult with his editors. On one occasion the city editor told him that he wanted to know when the President was going to sign an important bill for the District of Columbia so that they could cover the signing. Kilpatrick asked the press secretary who told him that President Johnson was going to wait until the Senate was back in session the following week. Kilpatrick reported this to the editor and the next day found out that Johnson had signed the bill that morning. "So I looked silly to the city desk," he said, "that wants to know why I can't tell them a little bit more about what he's going to do. And that happened over and over and over again, things of that sort."

Kilpatrick came to the *Post* in 1952 after a number of years as Washington correspondent for the *San Francisco Chronicle*, the *Chicago Sun-Times*, and the *Birmingham* (Alabama) *News*. He began his newspaper career in Birmingham, Alabama. He has been observing and writing about the Washington political scene for many years and from many perspectives. He has written editorials for the *Post*, covered the Agriculture Department, written about political campaigns, and reported on the Senate.

Covering the Hill, he thought, was in many ways more interesting than covering the White House. There was no famine on Capitol Hill. Congress has 535 members and "those people like to see reporters. Their life depends on their getting publicity and they like to talk when they're not working on top secret stuff. They're accessible; they understand reporters; there's action. If there isn't action in one committee, there's action in another."

The House press gallery is in the domed Capitol building on the Hill. Mary Russell, one of the *Post* reporters who covers the House is supposed to be there for an interview. She is late. Reporters are sitting on leather sofas reading newspapers. Some are talking on the telephone in pay telephone booths. At one end of the room are cubicles and typewriters. An old man wanders through the room selling peanuts in large brown paper bags. Some of the reporters greet him and buy some.

Finally Mary Russell appears, and apologizes for being late. "I had an appointment with a Congressman and he never showed up," she says. She is friendly, attractive, brown-haired, in her mid-thirties, seems earnest and sincere. She escorts her visitor downstairs to the basement cafeteria and talks over a Coke while dishes clatter in the background.

"How do you cover the House? Well, you get over here about nine thirty or so and probably you'll want to go to a committee hearing. There are 54 committees so you have to have a sense of what bill is due to come out. The hearings go on from ten o'clock until quarter of twelve. Then you come over from the House Office

Building to the Capitol. At five minutes to twelve Carl Albert, the Speaker of the House, has a press conference in his ornate office. There are usually one or two questions about what bill is going to be on the floor and something about the Presidential budget.

"At noon as soon as the prayer is over, you rush up to the gallery and they have what is known as a series of one-minute speeches. Sometimes they're as ludicrous as whether Notre Dame or North Carolina State won the basketball game last night. Some days they're using them to bring up some issue that they think hasn't been clearly heard, even sometimes blaming another Congressman for something that has happened. So even though rarely does a big news story come out of them, you should listen to the one-minute speeches.

"That's followed by whatever bill they happen to be taking up. Mondays and Tuesdays they work on District of Columbia bills which I'm not concerned with and Tuesday they work on what they call bills under suspension which have to be passed by a two-thirds vote and they're generally not controversial and not national in scope. So on those days you look for other things to do. And those things can be feature stories. These can be on new Congressmen or you might want to talk to some of the old Congressmen who are just retiring about how Congress has changed in the last 25 years.

"Generally the session recesses about five or six o'clock. Sometimes, it depends on the time, but usually I stay up here, write my stories in the press gallery and send them in by telecopier or Western Union or dictating and don't go down to the office. If I have enough time, I will go down to the office to pick up mail and write the story. Generally your copy is due in at seven thirty."

So it is usually eight o'clock before Mary Russell gets

home to the old town house near the Capitol which she and her husband gutted and restored themselves. To the question, "How did you find the time?" she replies casually, "Oh, I was working as an editor at that time. I worked from four o'clock to twelve thirty and I had a lot of time during the day to do it. But, you know, it was exhausting and once I did get it finished, decorated and everything, I haven't touched it since."

With both husband and wife working at demanding, high-pressure jobs, there isn't much time for anything else. "As my husband keeps saying," she laughs, "what one of us needs is a wife because we both get home about eight o'clock at night, tired, and by the time you fix something to eat and relax for a little bit, it's ten or eleven at night and time to go to bed. On weekends what we like to do best is play golf or walk in the woods, get away from it all. And I find myself instead of leisurely shopping or something, just running through stores, whether I'm buying groceries or clothes or whatever, just so it doesn't take too much time."

Mary Russell has been covering the House of Representatives for the *Post* since 1973. Ever since she came to Washington in 1965 as an editor in the women's section, she had been trying to get a political assignment.

"When I was a kid, when we first got our television set, the Kefauver hearings were on TV and that's the first thing I ever knew about things. Paul Douglas and Humphrey and Clark and Morse. There were a lot of kind of big names and personalities or at least I thought so in the 1950s. So I always liked Congress."

But being a well-informed outsider and knowing how Congress works, from the inside, well enough to cover it are two different matters.

"When I got to the House, I realized that despite the

fact that I was pretty well read and pretty interested, I had no idea how the place operated, no conception, absolutely none. And the first thing I learned was that the people whose names I read in the papers were not necessarily the people who ran the place and that people's conceptions of how it operates are just far off the mark."

So Russell sees her job as educating readers as well as reporting what goes on in the House day by day.

"We don't tell them what Congress does do, how it works as an institution. Those are very dull stories and nobody's terribly interested in them. But I kind of try from time to time to take it upon myself to do pieces about the institution and do stories about, for instance, a budget reform bill. There's really nothing more important than Congress taking control of the budget. Everything is touched by the budget. So I try to do stories on that.

"I try to do stories on the reforms. Right now they're changing the committee structure. The committee structure doesn't mean anything to most people. They know that there are committees and that they report out bills, but beyond that nothing. So I try to do stories about changing the committees."

She talks seriously, like a teacher. "I'd like to do a story about the House itself, that unlike the Senate individuals don't stand out, that coalitions are important. One guy said that the Senate is like a game of checkers and the House is like chess. It's a much more subtle and devious game, putting legislation through. I'd like to talk about that, about the fact that the House members consider themselves and, with some justification, better technicians; they know what's in their legislation and they're thoroughly versed in it."

If she didn't know how the House functioned when

she started the job, how did she learn? Her answer was quick.

"You talk to people. That's the job, constantly talking to people. Not the committee chairmen; they're not the ones who know the most. That's another phenomenon of this particular Congress. They traded very competent but dictatorial and tyrannical Southern committee chairmen, who generally died or were not reelected, for somewhat less competent, weaker, if more liberal committee chairmen. The committee chairmen are probably at the weakest point they have been. So who do I talk to. Suppose I'm interested in a particular bill. I would talk to the Representatives who are most actively for it and against it. I would talk to the White House. I'd talk to lobbyists for and against it. And I'd talk to committee staff members.

"And I also get a lot of press releases and phone calls from people saying, 'Hey, I think such and such a bill is a good story,' or 'Mr. So-and-so is going to make an important speech,' and I just exercise my judgment about whether it would be a good story or not."

Mary Russell pinpoints her interest in politics as starting in 1952 with the Kefauver hearings. Her interest in writing goes back even further, to when she was eight years old and wrote horse and dog stories which a little friend, who had artistic ambitions, illustrated. She went to Marquette University in Wisconsin, majored in journalism, and then went to work writing features for a Sunday newspaper in Evansville, Indiana. She was then made women's editor and, although she was not very happy to be working in a women's section, she stuck with the job for two years. Finally she decided that if she was going to work in a women's department she might as well aim for the top so she applied at the *Washington Post* and was hired as a makeup editor in the women's section. That meant supervising the printers who laid out the pages and other odds and ends, but soon after she arrived, the night women's editor left and Mary Russell got her job.

All the while she was trying to get a reporting assignment and finally in late 1967, she was given a chance. What was coming up was the 1968 political campaign which she covered from a women's point of view—interviews with candidates' wives and other political feature stories.

And 1968 was a year she will never forget. "I couldn't believe 1968. It started in March when I was supposed to go to the Romney campaign. The day I was supposed to go, he dropped out. So then they said, 'O.K., the Humphrey campaign,' so one night I was covering a Democratic dinner where Humphrey was speaking and Martin Luther King was dead. And the next day I was to have an interview with Mrs. Ronald Reagan and I went to the Madison Hotel and I'm up on the tenth floor and I'm watching Washington burn. And a month later I get on a plane and go out to Oregon and Oregon is this kind of watershed of the McCarthy campaign and all this idealism of young people and all that and California a week later and I'm standing in the kitchen and Bobby Kennedy is killed. I was in a state of shock."

Politics subsided and Russell became involved in the creation of a new section at the *Post* called Style—an amalgam of the women's section, the drama, music and art criticism, and other features. She was absorbed in the complexities of creating this section—first as a reporter, then as an editor—until 1972, another Presidential election year. This time she was given an assignment on the national desk covering politics and other subjects. After the election when the staff was reorganized, she was given her present beat.

The White House and the Capitol are probably the two top assignments in the country for a political reporter, the two centers for political action, crisis and drama, and the places where one sees the leading political personalities at work. The White House focuses around one person—the President—and reporters hang on every word he says or, failing that, they must be satisfied with what his staff tells them. On the Hill there is complexity, variety, a clash of personalities and political philosophies. The reporter has many more choices to make about what should be covered and what should not—what committee hearing to go to, which member of Congress to interview, which press release to follow up on. They are two very different beats, making different demands, requiring different reporting skills.

CHAPTER 5

Peeling an Onion
Down to the Core

*I*n the back of the newsroom a solitary, dark-haired figure is bent over a typewriter. It is eleven o'clock in the morning. Most reporters are out on assignment at this hour but Ronald Kessler got his assignment several months ago and is now typing a first draft of a series that will run for a week.

He sits hunched over the typewriter, his shoulders stiff. His coat is flung over his desk and his tie is loosened. He pauses, then pecks rapidly at the keys of the electric typewriter with his right forefinger. He is oblivious to the phones ringing and the people walking past him.

Ron Kessler is only thirty but he has been a reporter for ten years and is now one of the best investigative reporters in the business. He received the Polk award for two sets of articles he wrote in 1972: one series on illegal kickbacks and other abuses that increased settlement costs for homeowners in the Washington area and the other on conflicts of interest among trustees and administrators of Washington area hospitals. He has also worked on aspects of the Watergate story, mostly those dealing with income tax records and other financial matters.

The term "investigative reporting" is widely used and widely misunderstood. Some newspaper people think it is altogether redundant—all good reporters investigate and any reporter who does his or her job properly is an investigative reporter. But to Ron Kessler the term has a very specific meaning: "I do not define an investigative reporter as a person who gets an exclusive story based on a leak or fairly reputable information or a document that comes out of an agency. I think that's good reporting but it's not investigative reporting. Investigative reporting is digging much deeper than reporting on one particular document or what one particular person has said and really ferreting out the truth as much as anybody can do that, by using a number of techniques such as looking at a large number of documents, a large number of records, interviewing a large number of people, doing calculations based on the results that you come up with and generally, as the managing editor says, peeling an onion down to the core."

While other reporters are working on daily assignments and turning in stories every day or every few days, Kessler is turned loose for three or four months at a time to dig out a story that will usually amount to a series that runs for four or five days in the paper.

The phone rings, Kessler answers. It is the Washington postmaster. Kessler asks him a lot of questions about the procedure for sorting mail. He wants to know every detail, every step. He repeats a question, taking notes in a spiral stenographic notebook in an illegible scrawl that looks like shorthand. Then he reads back what he has written and asks the postmaster if he agrees that this is the procedure. "There won't be any dispute if somebody else says it's different?" he asks.

When asked about the story he is currently working on, he balks. He will only say that it is about the postal service—costs and services, why the costs have risen and service deteriorated, and whether costs have risen out of proportion to other costs in the country.

Kessler talks haltingly, guardedly, weighing each word. He is tight and controlled, not one to give away much of himself. Since he is used to questioning people who are reluctant to give up information, he seems to have learned to be cautious in answering questions himself.

He explains how the hospital story, published in 1972, began. "Another reporter got a tip from a source that he had had for a long time that some of the trustees of this hospital were involved in a conflict of interest. In this case the person said that the hospital has its bank accounts at a particular bank and that the balances are quite high and there's no interest paid and one of the trustees of the hospital is an officer of the bank. And I took it from there."

The story grew from one tip into a full-scale investigation of other conflicts of interest, how hospital financing is organized, and how totally unaccountable hospitals are to the public.

Some of the information which he got came from public records, such as the fact that one of the hospital trustees was also a bank officer. But most of the fact finding required hard digging. At least half of the people he contacted were unwilling to talk to him. But once he found a few people who would talk the story started coming together.

"Once you get one person in the institution who will talk to you," he said, "then he can give you other people who are likely to talk, maybe who've left the place and are no longer beholden to it, and you sort of have to feel out who the best possibilities might be. Eventually you get so much material that it becomes very easy and people will just start coming in to you over the door. Sometimes you have to keep them out but that doesn't happen unless you've first put in the hard work."

Those early weeks of a story—the weeks of making contacts that don't pan out, going down blind alleys, are frustrating and time-consuming. Sometimes the investigation does not materialize but Kessler tries to cover himself by gathering additional information along the way that can be used for other kinds of stories. For example, on the hospital story, while he was trying to substantiate conflicts of interest, he was also gathering information which could have been used for a feature story on how a hospital works or on the financing of hospitals.

Kessler can think of only one time when an investigation which he was doing did not materialize, where he could not substantiate his investigation.

"I was still able to do stories," he said, "but they weren't about the main point and they didn't reflect all the time that I'd spent on the story. You have to use a lot of judgment in selecting stories that you're going to spend time on. There are thousands of injustices that go on every day. You have to pick out ones that affect lots of people and that you have a good chance of pinning down with a reasonable amount of time."

Much of the information which Kessler needs comes from documents, sometimes publicly available reports and other material, but quite often they are confidential reports, memoranda, and records which he must get from his carefully cultivated sources. Once he has all the information, he must organize it, figure out what it all means, and put it into terms that will be clear to the readers of the newspaper.

Kessler has established an elaborate system of filing and indexing his information. He takes notes on filing cards of both his interviews and the most significant information from documents. Then he makes Xerox copies of the cards and files all the information alphabetically in a loose leaf binder so that he can flip through the pages easily to find a particular fact at a moment's notice. His indexing and cross-indexing allow him to see related facts at a glance and to amass substantial amounts of information when he is writing a story. He writes stories "rich in facts rather than opinions or just vaguely remembered conclusions."

Then he has to spend a lot of time comparing figures, discovering which ones are false or inflated, and re-working them into meaningful statistics.

"It's important to quantify and be as precise as possible when you're doing a story like that," Kessler says. "For example, it's one thing to say that they have interest-free accounts and that they're losing interest. It's another thing to actually figure out how much interest they could have gotten if they had invested it properly and then to convert that to how much each patient lost per day there as a result of this policy.

"It's also important to pin down just what is wrong with this practice. It's not enough to say that they have interest-free accounts or conflicts of interest. You have to go into what is a conflict of interest and is it illegal, cite the laws, if there are any, which pertain to it, which I did, or any other regulations that prohibit conflict of interest. And that makes all the difference as to the impact of a story. You have to burrow down as far as you can."

To complete an investigation in four months, Kessler has to put in an enormous amount of work to do all the interviewing, research, analysis, and writing required. "An investigative reporter has to put in a tremendous number of extra hours and become totally involved personally in what he is doing. Otherwise he might come up with a story once a year and that's not acceptable to anybody. It's just part of the job that you work nights and weekends and holidays and nobody knows what you're doing. You don't get overtime or extra time for it."

He explains why his kind of writing is so much more demanding than the average news story. "Every paragraph, instead of just being a quote from someone official, is maybe a result of talking to dozens and dozens of people, calculating all kinds of figures and reading maybe six congressional reports and five GAO [Government Accounting Office] reports."

Since he doesn't turn in a story every day like most reporters, Kessler establishes his own schedule. If he is in the writing stage of a story, he comes in to the newsroom about nine-thirty in the morning and leaves around six. If he is interviewing people, he may not come to the office at all but spend his whole day talking to people and then go home and make phone calls during the evening to people who do not want to be interviewed at their offices. Or he may spend evenings reading reports or memos of Congressional hearings or, as he puts it, "calculating all the rip-offs with my electronic calculator."

Kessler has a wife and two young children and he is a bit defensive when asked how much time he is able to spend with them. "When I'm working at home, I can spend some time with the kids," he says. "They come in and ask for the stapler or something and I try to devote enough time to them. This job does take a lot of time but then I cut down on other outside activities. I don't go bowling or play cards or even engage in sports which I should do, and I try to be very patient with them."

He is so involved in his work that he doesn't even think about getting away from it very much. At social gatherings he doesn't mind talking shop with other journalists or friends in other professional fields. He does manage to shed his responsibilities once in a while when he takes his family on vacation for a few weeks. Otherwise, leisure time comes at the beginning of a story when he hasn't gotten completely involved and isn't working twelve hours a day on it.

One might expect that an investigative reporter would get himself into situations where he was threatened because of things he had written or harassed in some way. Kessler is sanguine about this aspect of his job. He recalls one threat. "After one story I did, a person called me and told me he'd punch me in the nose. It wasn't a pleasant experience to be on the receiving end of such a threat." But the threat was not carried out. He also recalls that on a few occasions people have offered him large gifts, such as a car, if he would withhold information. He has never been followed and he does not know whether his telephone is tapped. "I always assume that my line might be tapped," he said, "but there's not much you can do about it."

Although direct threats and bribe attempts are not too frequent, there are other unpleasant aspects of Kessler's job, which require him to be tough-skinned in the face of insults and refusals of people to be interviewed. When his seven-part series on the operations of the Postal Service appeared, he wrote a sidebar (a short piece accompanying the main article) describing some of the difficulties in getting information out of Postal Service officials. For example, when he tried to tour a new bulk mail sorting building in Jersey City, N.J., he was turned away by guards at the gate. No less than six top postal officials refused to talk to him; while interviewing the then Postmaster General Elmer T. Klassen, he was berated and told, "All you're really trying to do is smear the Postal Service, including Klassen." Finally, James H. Byrne, the postal staff member in charge of public information, denied that the Postal Service had been uncooperative and in a letter accused Kessler of "unprofessional and unethical tactics" and charged that he had vowed "to hold us up to ridicule in his story if we did not jump at his commands." Executive editor Benjamin Bradlee denied the charges.

Bradlee's defense of Kessler brings up an important point about the role of the editors, their willingness to back up a reporter, and their commitment to what a reporter is working on. Kessler feels that this kind of commitment is one of the things that makes it possible to do good investigative reporting at the *Post*.

"You have editors who are not only willing to spend the time," he says, "but who really want to know the truth, who really get excited about pulling away the cloud of deception, misleading statements that cover up a lot of the things that we read about in the paper. Since you need to be off on your own for several months without much contact with any human beings except the people you're investigating, every now and then you need some little charge from the editors you're working with. You want to feel that they're interested and that they're behind you. And then another thing, of course, which is almost taken for granted, is editors supporting you in the face of threats and in the face of other complaints."

The public support of reporters is preceded by relentless cross examination from the editors to make sure that every statement that is written is absolutely accurate. Harry Rosenfeld is a taskmaster. After all, his reputation is on the line if a reporter is caught in a false or misleading statement. "For example," he says, "on the Watergate, or the hospital series by Kessler, we'd meet with the reporters and possibly one or more other editors and go over the stories line by line by line. Who said this? Where did this come from? We asked hard questions and they either had hard answers or went out and got hard answers—or we took it out. When we were satisfied and if libel was a possibility, we called the lawyers. They did the same thing."

Kessler is not very concerned about the legal problem of being sued for libel. What he considers much more serious is the issue of confidentiality of sources, which is at the heart of freedom of the press. Newspapers are fighting to defend this relationship which gives reporters the same kind of confidentiality privilege that doctors and lawyers have, a privilege which is essential if people who ask that their statements be off the record are to continue to talk to reporters and keep accurate information flowing to the public.

Kessler's problem with confidentiality came about when he did a second hospital story about another hospital with interest-free bank accounts and conflicts of interest among members of the board of trustees. After the story appeared, the hospital was sued for these practices and lawyers for the hospital wanted to take a deposition from Kessler and subpoena his notes. The *Post*'s lawyers filed a request with the judge that the request of the hospital's lawyers not be granted and the judge granted the request.

When you listen to Kessler talk, you get a sense of a person who goes about his business with a kind of dogged determination to get to the bottom of things. He is steady, self-confident, low-key, but there is a fire burning inside him which keeps him going after the truth. He doesn't see his stories as crusades; as a matter of fact, he considers it very dangerous to become emotionally involved in a story on one side or the other. "The result will not be a dispassionate account," he says. "It will probably be one-sided and you don't want that because then the target of the investigation can come back the next day with a very compelling defense. I'd rather have the defense in the story."

Kessler has been a reporter since he was in junior high school and he sees those reportorial qualities of trying to dispel myths and get to the bottom of things as basic parts of his personality. He started out working on the school paper, even then writing long, in-depth stories and conducting surveys. Then he went to college at Clark University in Worcester, Massachusetts, and spent most of his time working on the student newspaper. He conducted opinion surveys on social regulations, curfews, and visiting hours in girls' dormitories, and then began to get into bigger issues like housing discrimination against black students.

While he was still a student, he got a part-time job on the *Worcester Telegram*, covering, as he puts it, "the very lowest things that you cover in journalism, sewer board meetings and accidents." He finally dropped out of college altogether, worked six more months for the *Telegram* and was hired by the *Boston Herald* as a night police reporter.

Kessler does not regret having left college without a degree. He felt that he could get whatever education he wanted on his own and that reporting events, interviewing the makers of history, was much more satisfying than reading textbooks.

At the *Herald* he covered night police for only eight months before he began to get into investigative reporting. At first he had to do investigations on his own, fitting them in between his regular assignments. After he had proved himself, he began to be given investigative assignments on a more regular basis. He did some articles on American Telephone and Telegraph's practice of monitoring people's telephone calls to check quality of service and a few reforms resulted from this exposure. He also did a 25-part series on the Boston public school system and wrote editorials.

After three years in Boston he went to work for the *Wall Street Journal* in New York. There he specialized in investigative reporting and won a number of awards. One of his big stories was about the largest wholesale distributor of magazines on the East Coast who had Mafia connections and was making threats against a number of publications, including Time, Inc. Although the *Wall Street Journal* was itself distributed by this company, the paper did not flinch from publishing the story. But there was no retribution.

Kessler stayed at the *Wall Street Journal* for two years and went from there to the *Post*. This move from the *Journal* to the *Post* has been a very fortunate one for him, and Kessler apparently has no regrets about the change. He says he has no desire to be anywhere else or be doing anything but what he is doing now. He likes investigative reporting; he likes working conditions at the *Post*; the salary is good (experienced reporters at the *Post* make over $20,000 a year); he doesn't even want to write a book, although a series of his articles could easily be expanded into a book-length manuscript.

"If I got enough money so that it would be impossible to refuse," he says, "I guess I might do it. But I don't see any great advantage to a book over this. Writing a series in the *Post* gets to far more readers than a book would, I think. The *Post*'s circulation is roughly 600,000 and they frequently run my stories on the news wire which goes to 350 newspapers. So the circulation is millions and millions."

Good working conditions, good salary, esteem from his colleagues, wide readership: what more does a reporter need? For the moment, at least, Ron Kessler can't think of anything more.

CHAPTER 6

From Middletown to Middle Europe

When Dan Morgan was a student at Harvard in the late 1950s, he had no burning ambition to be a newspaper reporter. He majored in English but he didn't write for the *Harvard Crimson*, and after he graduated he spent a year working his way around the world on Scandinavian merchant ships. After a year and a half with the army in Germany, he came back home with a desire to work on a newspaper.

He first applied to the *New York Times* and was told politely to come back in a year after he had had some experience. Then, setting his sights a little lower, he went to Hackensack, New Jersey, just outside of New York City. At the *Hackensack Record* he was bluntly and abruptly turned down. He also received a rude turndown from the *Boston Globe* and was beginning to get completely discouraged about the newspaper business. Then a friend told him about a small paper in Middletown, Connecticut, which was owned and run by two young brothers. So Morgan went off to Middletown for an interview. Derry D'Oench, the editor, was interested. A few days later he offered Morgan a job, not in the main office in Middletown, but, because he lacked experience, he was sent "down-county" for seasoning.

For a year Morgan was the southern Middlesex County bureau chief for the *Middletown Press*. He would start out in the afternoon interviewing the selectmen and the town clerks of the small towns of Essex, Deep River, and Chester. Then he would go home for supper and in the evening go off to a meeting of the Board of Selectmen or the Board of Education or some other community organization. When the meeting broke up about midnight, he would go back to the bureau and compose three or four stories on an open telex line to Middletown. His four or five thousand words of copy would appear in the morning paper, more or less unchanged.

This routine continued for about a year. Then, having proved himself, he was brought back to Middletown, where he worked for about a year. One day when he was interviewing Douglass Cater, who was at the Center for Advanced Studies at Wesleyan University on a one-year leave of absence from the *Reporter* magazine, Cater suggested that he ought to think about working for a newspaper in Washington called the *Washington Post*. Morgan had never seen a copy of the *Post*, but he dutifully called up for an interview, went down to Washington, and saw Al Friendly, the managing editor, and Ben Gilbert, the city editor. A few days later, Gilbert offered him a job.

Morgan has a vivid recollection of that phone conversation with Gilbert in 1963.

Gilbert: Well, got a job for you. Be here in a week.

Morgan: That's very interesting. What will I be doing?

Gilbert: Reporting.

Morgan: Could you be a little more specific?

Gilbert: No. Do you want the job or don't you?

Morgan: Well, can I have two weeks?

Gilbert: I don't want to give it to you but I will. Two weeks. It's the most I've ever given anybody.

So with that introduction Morgan came to the *Post* as a city reporter, working from six o'clock in the evening until two in the morning, covering night police. He recalls the shift from the *Middletown Press*, with a circulation of 20,000, to the *Washington Post* as a traumatic experience.

"It was a little like being inducted into the army," he said. "You had the same sense of awe and loss and confusion. It was like being inducted in as a buck private."

He remembers walking into the newsroom late one night looking very depressed and being told by the night city editor, "Morgan, why are you looking so depressed? Nobody's shooting for your job."

At that time starting from the bottom was the only way to get a job at the *Post*. Many of today's top editors and reporters were colleagues of Morgan's on the night police beat: Lee Lescaze, the foreign editor; Lon Tuck, assistant managing editor of the Style section; and Bob Kaiser, the correspondent in the Soviet Union. Now, under Bradlee, people are hired for high level jobs, but in those days, as Morgan puts it, "there was no lateral entry."

From the night police beat he went to the D.C. courts and covered drunkenness, juvenile delinquency, and landlord and tenant cases. By 1965 Ben Bradlee had replaced Al Friendly as managing editor and he had started an experiment, sending reporters out for short tours in Vietnam. In 1967 Morgan was chosen to go to Vietnam for three months and had his ticket in his pocket when Bradlee called him into his office and said, "How would you like to go to Bonn instead?"

He was being given a long-term assignment since Anatole Shub, who had been in Bonn, had obtained a visa to the Soviet Union and was reopening the *Post*'s bureau in Moscow. Morgan guesses that Bradlee plucked him from his city reporter's beat to give other reporters mired in D.C. politics a sense of hope, a feeling that they too could move on to something else.

Perhaps Bradlee was also remembering his own experience as a young police reporter at the *Post* in the late 1940s, feeling that he was going nowhere. He finally left the paper and took a job as press attaché at the U.S. Embassy in Paris. Now nearly twenty years later he was looking at a young Harvard English major, as he had been, a man fluent in German, as he is fluent in French, a bright young reporter stuck in what seemed like a dead-end job. Maybe Bradlee just wanted to give Morgan the chance that he wasn't given.

So Dan Morgan went to Bonn to cover Germany and sometimes other areas excluding England and the Soviet Union. In Europe 1967 was a quiet year but then came 1968. First the Czech spring when Dubcek, the liberal prime minister, took over the government and began to open up Czechoslovakia; then a West European monetary crisis; then the April and May student demonstrations in Paris which led to a succession of strikes and the toppling of de Gaulle's government; then more student demonstrations in Berlin and the shooting of Rudi Dütschke, the New Left leader; finally in August came the Soviet invasion of Czechoslovakia and the rolling back of all the liberal reforms. It was a rough breaking-in period for a fledgling foreign correspondent.

Morgan spent a good part of the year shuttling back and forth between Bonn and Prague. "Whenever something happened in Bonn, I'd be in Prague and whenever something was happening in Prague, I'd be in Bonn," is the way he recalls it. His experience during that year showed the *Post* editors that they could not continue to operate without a bureau in Eastern Europe. In 1970 Morgan opened an Eastern European bureau based in Belgrade, Yugoslavia, where he stayed until 1973. Then he came back to Washington to work on the national desk, covering international politics in Washington.

Morgan is a tall, slim, handsome man in his mid-thirties, who wears stylish aviator glasses and suits with fitted waists and long jackets. When he walks off the elevator into the fifth floor newsroom with his tan trenchcoat billowing behind him, he looks like the classic stereotype of the foreign correspondent. Give him another ten years or so and he will look distinguished, with grey sideburns and a deep voice.

His two European assignments were a study in contrast. In Bonn he was living in a comfortable modern house with his German wife and two school-age children; in Belgrade it took him months to find a five-room apartment with no central heating and a hot water heater that worked intermittently. In Bonn his office was in a building owned by Reuters, the British press agency, with all the facilities he needed for filing his copy by telex; in Belgrade he worked in the basement of his home until a flood drove him to seek other quarters and it took him many months to obtain a telex machine. In Bonn he had a good background in the language of the country; in Belgrade he had to wrestle with a difficult Slavic language that was completely new to him.

In spite of his difficulties there, Morgan speaks about Belgrade with great enthusiasm. Perhaps because life there was so different from anything he had experienced before, it offered him a challenge which he had not had anywhere else. He found Belgrade a fascinating place, whereas Bonn was comfortably dull and provincial.

In Bonn it is so easy to get information that a correspondent can become very lazy. There are at least three press conferences a week with important government officials which all the reporters, German and foreign, may attend. Some reporters simply depend on press conferences and government handouts for their stories. But it does not take much digging to get information in Bonn. Morgan characterizes the German government as "the leakiest government in Europe" and Bonn as an excellent place to pick up information about what is going on all over the continent.

When he was ready to file a story, he simply went downstairs to the Reuters office with his typed copy and gave it to a telex operator. The operator retyped the story on the telex machine, which transmitted the story to a communications center in London. From there it went directly to the *Post*'s foreign desk in Washington.

If Morgan filed at the end of his working day, six or seven o'clock in the evening, his copy would reach Washington about two o'clock in the afternoon, since there is a six-hour time difference between Europe and the East Coast. The time difference made it tempting to file later and later in the evening because he could file at midnight and still be in time for the Washington deadline. It also gave editors the opportunity to call him at two o'clock in the morning to ask questions about his copy or send him to cover a late breaking story that they had just gotten in from the wire services.

When he first arrived in Bonn he worked very hard to perfect his German. He hired a German university student to converse with him for an hour a day. This not only gave him practice in the language but also gave him an opportunity to learn about what was going on in the country in an informal way—what students were thinking, what plays and movies and art exhibits were going on, what jokes people were telling.

Morgan and his family lived in a house in a comfortable suburb of the city, in an area where many of the prominent German politicians lived. His son went to an international school for Americans and other English-speaking children and his daughter went to a German school. His wife was happy to be in her own country. There were few complaints except about the weather—hot and muggy in summer and grey, damp, and misty in winter.

After this comfortable existence, Belgrade was a shock. Morgan could have chosen to base himself in Vienna where life would have been easier but he felt that if he were going to be covering the Communist countries of Eastern Europe, he should be living in one, to have a feel for what was going on there and how people lived.

First of all there was a terrible housing shortage in Belgrade. The place he finally managed to get was half a villa in a suburb near downtown Belgrade, which he shared with his landlady and her daughter and son-in-law.

For an intense and enthusiastic reporter, apartment hunting and other time-consuming chores like getting a car registered and getting household goods through customs were enormous frustrations. He wanted to be out filing stories, not standing in line at some government office.

Morgan had a large territory to cover from Belgrade —Poland, Czechoslovakia, Hungary, Rumania, Bulgaria, Yugoslavia, Greece, and sometimes Turkey and Cyprus. It was impossible to learn all the languages, so he had to depend on interpreters. In Belgrade he began studying Serbo-Croatian as soon as he arrived and he hired office assistants who could translate the local papers into English for him. Before he left, he had reached the point where he could at least read enough Serbo-Croatian to decide what he wanted to have translated.

In the other countries he often depended on interpreters. Sometimes reporters or friends referred him to local people who were willing to spend a few days with him, not only interpreting when he interviewed people or visited a factory or collective farm, but also providing invaluable insights into local life—plays, films, books—things that he would not find out from government press digests in English or from the U.S. Embassy staff.

When he was not covering breaking stories, which were rare during the three years he spent in Belgrade, he tried to write stories comparing aspects of life in a number of countries. He would travel to all the East European countries, for example, and collect information on agriculture or economics or cultural life and then return to Belgrade to write a story about all the countries he had visited. In December 1972 Morgan and Bob Kaiser, the Moscow correspondent, switched places. Morgan traveled through the Soviet Union and Kaiser came to Eastern Europe. They came back to Belgrade together and wrote a twelve-part series comparing the two areas.

Being a foreign correspondent means that you are always on the job. Everything that happens to you may be material for a story—where and how you shop for groceries, what movies you see, what restaurants you go to, what you talk about when you have dinner at a friend's house, and whom your children play with.

As Morgan puts it, "When you're a foreign correspondent, you've got to wake up and want to do a story. No one is going to tell you what to write. You have to be a self-starter. You've got to be unhappy if you're not working."

Even when he went on vacation, he was contributing to the beat. He and his family usually went on camping trips and met Greeks, Bulgarians, and Yugoslavs at the various campsites where they stayed. Morgan always had a notebook and pencil in his pocket and usually ended up writing a piece about his travels.

Sometimes the job made even more direct demands on him. Whenever he went anywhere he had to let the foreign desk in Washington know where he was and he listened to the news on the car radio several times a day so that he would know if anything had happened that he had to cover. Once he was asleep in his tent in a campsite in Greece when he heard a voice outside calling him to the telephone. He groggily followed the proprietor of the campsite to his house, picked up the phone and there was the foreign editor in Washington on the line telling him that Secretary of State Rogers was going to be making a tour of Eastern Europe. Would Morgan go to Athens to meet him and go with the party to Bucharest, Budapest, and Belgrade? Morgan left the next morning for Athens and his wife drove the two children and the camping gear back to Belgrade.

Adjusting to life in Belgrade was not easy but learning to live in Washington again after six years overseas was a big problem for Morgan too. Nevertheless, he felt that he had to make the adjustment. "It's a mistake to stay away too long," he said. "I think if you spend too much time away, you really begin to lose touch with your country and I think I needed to come back."

Soon after his return the *Post* sent him around the country to collect his impressions and write a piece for "Outlook," the Sunday news supplement. "When you first come back," Morgan said, "you have a couple of months when you really see your own country almost as a foreigner and you have observations which are fresh and sharp."

73

After his time in the closed and suspicious countries of Eastern Europe he was struck by the openness in the United States. People were willing to give him their telephone numbers; he was not asked for identification when he checked in at a hotel; people openly named particular politicians as crooks without lowering their voices or looking over their shoulders before speaking. On the other hand, he was struck by some of the similarities of the economies of Eastern Europe and the United States. Eastern European countries were bringing in technology and capitalist marketing techniques from the West while the market economy of the United States was experiencing some of the irrational shortages which had long plagued Eastern Europe. He was also aware of freer, more informal life styles and such things as massage parlors and porno shops which he had become accustomed to in Germany but was surprised to find in Denver, Colorado.

It was difficult to adjust to working in Washington too. When he was a foreign correspondent there was no one around to tell Morgan what to do every day. For the most part, he decided what stories he was going to write, when he was going to travel, where he was going to go. The *Post* sent him a sum of money to run his office and he disbursed the funds himself and sent the *Post* an accounting. ("One spends a great deal of time submitting expense accounts. It's not one of the more glamorous parts of being a foreign correspondent," Morgan said.)

Back in Washington he suddenly felt cut down to size, "just another soldier." He now had a rather specialized mandate, covering international politics, and his working day ended when he left the office at night. Morgan does not want to be put into a box, he wants to be open to stimuli, to write about many things.

"I don't want to become a specialist," he says.

Another reason for coming back, he feels, is to stay in touch with the organization he is working for. "I think it's important to understand the paper," he said. "This organization has changed and grown immeasurably so that you have to come back here and work here and see what their problems are. Then if you go abroad again, you're a little more sympathetic to their problems."

And he does want to go abroad again. He is not sure where or when but he thinks it is important to have a complete change periodically, "be freshened up, have your mind flushed out now and then, change your environment completely."

Meanwhile, he keeps working and thinking and wondering about the choices which one must make to survive in a large organization like the *Post* where the pace is killing and competition is very rough. Washington is full of successful men who have sacrificed families and friends and ultimately themselves to get to the top. Morgan has reached the point in his career where he is clearly a successful reporter. Now he has to decide what his values are, where he wants to go, and how he is going to get there.

CHAPTER 7

The Noisy Stepchild

"*T*here are much greater withdrawal symptoms than I thought," says Martie Zad sadly. Zad was until recently the editor of the sports pages of the *Washington Post*. His new assignment is to explore the new technology that is revolutionizing newspaper production. "Somewhere along the line someone gave me credit as being a good administrator, good at organization," Zad says, "but it's tough going to a game on Sunday afternoon, watching it and knowing all the time that you're not going to have a say in what's going to be written."

From high school Zad went to the University of Maryland on a football scholarship but gave up playing early in his college career. Still on a scholarship, he went to work in the school's Athletic Department, in the public relations office. In Zad, the school newspaper found an avid sports reporter while in the newspaper Zad found the perfect profession.

The *Post*'s reporters covering the University got to know Zad and when a man was out sick in the sports section they called him to fill in, answering the phone and generally helping out for a week or so. "The fellow who was sick was out for over a year with a heart problem," Zad explains. "When he came back I was a sportswriter for the *Washington Post*, have been ever since. I was very fortunate because most graduates at that time were being sent to small papers for a few years. By the time I graduated I had three years' experience on the *Post*."

After deciding that he was going to be a sportswriter, Zad took full advantage of his college education to prepare himself. Though he switched his major to journalism, his instinctive wisdom directed him to take as many athletic coaching courses as would fit his program. Learning about football, basketball, baseball and other sports was as important as learning to write. As he puts it, "I'm sure none of those people who handled my copy in those early years would have labeled me a great writer or figured I was a great threat to Red Smith or Shirley Povich* but they surely were confident that I knew what I was talking about. If you go to a football game and know exactly what happened on the field and know why, the writing isn't so frightening."

Zad's long experience in the sports department makes him an excellent choice to mesh the new complicated technology with the intensely personal journalism that is practiced at the *Post*. In many ways, the sports section is a newspaper within a newspaper. International, national, and local sports news is covered from World Cup soccer to professional and college sports all over the country to local high school and sub-high school events. Sporting events are announced on the sports page as movies, plays, and concerts are listed other places in the paper. For many readers the racing results are the equivalent of the financial page. "So we have a little bit of everything," Zad says. "We do our own makeup so we have a news desk. We have our own photographer and picture desk. Our columnists, of course, are our editorial writers. Any guy who does try five or six jobs in the sports section and works his way

* Shirley Povich, dean of the *Post*'s sportswriters, was with the newspaper for fifty-two years before he retired last year. He recently came out of retirement to cover the Ali-Foreman fight in Zaire for the paper.

up has got a taste of the whole business of newspa-
pering."

As part of a larger paper, the sports section tends to
parallel the attitudes of the whole. In the past the
emphasis was on hard news; scores and the salient facts
were put in the lead paragraph. Zad admits to stealing a
line from one of his old editors, Russ Wiggins, when he
says, "The reader is entitled to one clean, clear whack at
the facts, and then you can dazzle him with your
adverbs and adjectives."

Though analytical journalism has been around a long
time, it was a generation of reporters who wanted to
understand the whys of what they were writing about
that put it in vogue. They saw themselves as writers as
well as reporters. Today it's difficult to separate the
columns, features, and think pieces from straight sports
news. Zad is a little sad about this. "The young reporter
does a basketball story, goes out to see the game, and
starts his piece with his thoughts of the game. Then he
does an interview with one of the players. You get all
this long before you find out who won the game, the
score or who was high scorer. No, they're brought along
too fast and they're all mixed up about what reporting a
sports event is all about."

This criticism does not stem from a nostalgia for the
good old days. Zad does not lament the passing of the
hero-worshipping reporter of yesteryear. He cites an
example of this kind of starry-eyed reporting. The
Mickey Mantle image created by reporters was a
smiling, wonderful athlete who hit home runs and ate
Wheaties. But after Mantle retired Jim Bonton wrote a
book giving the inside picture of his life as a ball player,
including his carousing and drinking. "This was the real
Mickey Mantle," Zad comments, "yet dozens of news-
papermen covered the Yankees for years but somehow

none of this ever got into the papers. I think that if something like that happened today a reporter would get reemed out if he didn't write the story."

Especially since Watergate, investigative reporting has become an important form of journalism, even in the sports department. Recently a top football writer and a science writer teamed up to study injuries of professional football players. They investigated hundreds of injuries, compared statistics, researched court cases, and interviewed people. The resulting series was highly successful for the *Post* and it is hoped that it made some impression on the people in the pro football game. Zad sees many other areas where this kind of coverage would be fruitful. He points especially to the franchise systems and financial practices of professional sports and to the bureaucracy that controls the American amateur athlete and the Olympics. Still Zad is realistic and sees that "the hard news is still your bread and butter. Four columnists are your next biggest thing. The rest comes when there is the space."

When Zad was the sports editor he usually came into the newsroom sometime after lunch and stayed through the evening hours to be on hand when the sports news was breaking. The sports section at the *Post* is a maze of cubby holes and desks set off in an area by itself on the fifth floor. There are a number of television sets available so the staff can watch some sports events. Zad's first chore was checking on assignments and finding out the kinds of stories he could expect from the reporters in the field. As the stories came in, he started to put the section together. He gauged his space, decided which stories to run and which to hold a day or so. Some stories had to be trimmed. Recycling stories (running the same story that appeared in the late edition the previous night in the day's early edition) had to be considered. "Everything would be set and you go downstairs for a sandwich and a cup of coffee," says Zad. "When you get back everything is disjointed. The Rams have traded someone to the Packers, and Meredith is going to the Giants, or the Yankees traded Mercer to San Francisco for Bobby Borid, who knows what else. At five thirty you had a section ready to go and now . . . so you tear the page down and start to redo it."

Zad feels a good editor has to be flexible. He is wise enough to know it isn't always the editor who makes the right decision. "Sometimes it can be to his advantage to be off," said Zad with a wry smile. "Some young imaginative guy who really got a feel for a story comes through. Sometimes it's dumb luck. A little oddity that moves out of somewhere and you give it a prominent little box on page one will brighten up the whole page."

The principal interests of the *Post*'s sports staff are the college and professional teams located in the D.C. area like the Redskins, Maryland, Navy, Virginia and Howard. Coverage of the national scene depends upon the importance of the event, as well as money and manpower. It's the editor's job to juggle all those ingredients to give a full, well-balanced, and responsible picture of what is happening in the sports world. He will deploy his staff to its best advantage and assign particular stories, but Zad points out, "For an editor sitting in his office with three blank walls and a window to say what he wants in the paper the next day is okay, but a good reporter out in the field is the one to know the story possibilities, and a good editor has to put his trust in the reporter's ability to get it." Zad likes a reporter who will fight for a story he believes in. It's usually a story the editor would never think of.

One reason for shifting staff assignments is to prevent

writers from getting stale. Zad obviously speaks with personal knowledge when he says, "Take a little town like Carlisle, Pennsylvania, where the Redskins do their training. Chain a guy in there, in a sort of hostile atmosphere—the players and coaches don't want anything to do with the press at that time. They're just there to get ready for the season and have too much work to do to give interviews or be questioned. After eight weeks of that you may have to pick him up in a strait-jacket."

The hiring talent of a sports editor can be his most important asset. A year or more may pass with no openings in the department, and then within a period of a few months there may be three slots to fill. If the editor doesn't bring in people with the right attitude, enthusiasm, and skills for the job, the section will not grow. On the other hand, if the right people are hired everyone's job is easier, the new reporter will develop more rapidly and the improvement in the section will be noticeable.

Finding these people is almost a full-time job. When a slot opens up the editor has to know quickly what kind of talent is available and where it is. While he was sports editor, Zad was constantly looking through smaller papers (the training ground of the newspaper business) for bright, inventive reporters. He often asked his staff about the reporters in the field. He wanted to know their attitudes, their abilities, and how they related to their jobs.

If Zad was interested in hiring a certain reporter, he would not ask him to send in samples of his work. Eight or ten of the best pieces done over a two-year period would tell nothing. Zad wanted to know what his work was like day in and day out. He wanted to see the reporter at his worst as well as at his best, so he would read the reporter's paper for at least a month. If he was still impressed he would call the prospective candidate to Washington, and the personal negotiations would begin.

It is much more difficult to get a good copy editor or makeup man than a reporter. They aren't as flexible, as eager to pack all their belongings and move their families. But they are needed on every staff, so for a sports editor, filling these openings can be a problem.

Writing for the sports section can be a shortcut to big league journalism. While in the other sections of the paper, a reporter could be on a local beat for years, a young sports reporter assigned to a local high school could soon be writing about the college scene, and within a year could be covering a pro team on a national basis. Zad feels that "when you decide to move out of sports, you can move out on an upper level. Many top columnists and commentators, the Westbrook Peglers and Ring Lardners, there are many of them, all started in sports. There used to be a joke around the office about the political analyst who used to be a sportswriter, and still was."

It has been twenty-eight years since Jackie Robinson came into the major leagues, and it has taken that long for baseball to have its first Black manager. Zad doesn't think it will take that long, but a woman sports editor is still in the distant future. Even in the male chauvinist world of sports it takes a bright young newspaperman ten years to become a columnist, and fifteen to become an editor. Zad feels it will take at least that long for a woman to mature enough in the business to be able to handle the complex problems of being a sports editor. It is only recently that women have been working in the sports section at all.

Nancy Scannell joined the *Post*'s sports staff about

two years ago. Zad is particularly enthusiastic about her ability and recalls her story about women in sports as being especially complex and effective. She checked the budgets of colleges and high schools and compared monies alloted for men's and women's sports. She also explored the opportunities that were available for women in athletics. Just as there are more women interested in sports today, so there are more women attracted to the sports staffs of national newspapers.

The Washington area does not have a surplus of small daily suburban newspapers, so the *Post* has tried to fill the needs of those communities. It is not only the largest paper in the capital, it is the largest daily in both Maryland and Virginia. There has been a great change in readership habits recently, especially in sports. More people are watching national sports on television while attendance at local sandlot and high school games has been diminishing. The sports section reflects this trend in reader interest.

Though readership habits is a major cause for less local sports coverage, it is by no means the only one. There are over a hundred high schools in the area covered by the *Post*'s circulation. If all sporting events were covered, the readership interest in each game would be indeed small. With the high costs of newsprint and production, the *Post* has to be very selective about what is published. And though the *Post* tries to keep up with the local sports scene, it cannot satisfy every avid parent who has a son or daughter competing in a local high school.

Zad feels particularly fortunate that his wife understands the business he's in. Her father was a journalist. Zad put into words what a reporter's wife has to go through: "He could get home around midnight and tell her he was assigned to the Penn Relays in Philadelphia at nine that morning. When was he coming home she would want to know. The Relays end Saturday evening at five and he should be home around ten that evening. This is unless the boss assigns him to a pro game on Sunday. Sure enough there is a call Friday night in his hotel room informing him he's due in New York for the Sunday Giant game. It's not unusual for a two-day trip to become a five-day stint."

Zad calls the spirit in the sports department "camaraderie and a get alongness. Over the years sports has been a stepchild so far as most of the other people in the paper were concerned. We were those guys back there always making noise and laughing. But more and more they're taking us serious. Editors, people in charge of personnel and morale have begun to realize what a vital section it is for the total product."

The attitudes of the new sports editor will be important not only to the sports section, but to the whole paper. He is Donald Edward Graham, the son of the publisher.

Graham has been the sports editor since August 1974. Before that he held many jobs at both the *Post* and *Newsweek* magazine. His first job was as a Metro reporter, and then he did layout and makeup on the news desk. On the business side he did budgets in the accounting department, worked in circulation, sold ads, and served as assistant production manager.

Before coming into the family business, Graham was an officer on the Washington police force. His year and a half experience there has been very useful. As he says, "Sometimes when I was covering demonstrations [for the *Post*] it was helpful to have contacts in the police department. And my experience as a policeman gave me some idea of who lives in the city and what kinds of stories are out there."

Standing in shirt sleeves with loosened tie, Graham blends into the newsroom scene. He is in his early thirties, over six feet tall, well-built, and athletically quick. When asked by an assistant editor if a certain reporter should cover an event, Graham answers, "Dynamite. Don't you think so? Isn't this his day off? Okay, we'll give him Saturday off." In that quick response he displays his respect for what his assistant thought, his sensitivity to the reporter, and his ability to react quickly.

"I think the challenge of an administrative job is not to be taken over by administrative detail," Graham says. His first consideration as sports editor is what appears in print, "to tell the people what they want to know and a little of what they didn't know they want to know."

He gives as an example of this challenge a recent piece on sports recruiting in high schools. Recruiting practices of colleges are accepted, but "now high schools are competing for junior high school athletes, seventh and eighth grade kids. Public, parochial, and some very prestigious private schools are doing it. They're offering money and special deals." Graham considers this kind of analytic reporting to be the sports section's responsibility to its readers.

When told that Martie Zad considered staff recruitment the most important function of a sports editor, Graham replies, "I'm sure glad he did. We have an excellent staff and I'm the beneficiary of Martie's smart hiring."

CHAPTER 8

Science as News

*T*om O'Toole is a science reporter. One doesn't necessarily think of science as hard news or of a science reporter under the pressure of daily deadlines like a city reporter. But the *Post*'s definition of subjects covered by a science reporter includes energy and in covering energy stories Tom O'Toole is one of the busiest reporters on the paper.

O'Toole is a short, stocky man of forty with a square, bulldog-like face and a seemingly aggressive manner; underneath the brusque exterior he is a friendly and helpful person.

His desk, piled high with magazines, journals, reports, newsletters, and other documents, is a landmark in the newsroom. Every once in a while he has to rake off the top of the pile and stack the papers in boxes because of complaints from Mrs. Graham and Bradlee about untidiness and fire hazard. The fire hazard problem is no joke. An arsonist once set a small fire in the back of the newsroom, and little blazes have occasionally broken out amongst the cluttered papers on chain-smoking reporters' desks.

The piles of reading material on O'Toole's desk are an indication of what he is up against as a science reporter—masses of information to be considered, sifted, digested, and either rejected or pursued as potential stories. Not only are there masses of written material to be assimilated but there is also a variety of people who can be consulted about numerous potential stories on oil, strip mining, atomic energy, and the space program, all of which are parts of Tom O'Toole's beat.

"That's the hardest part of the job," O'Toole says. "Using the time properly. What's important; what isn't. Not only what to write about but what to even look into. You have to have a good nose for news. In the science department nobody can tell you what's news. You have to tell them. In that way it's a great job. You're more independent than anybody around here because you're telling them what's important."

Science is a subject which cannot be ignored by newspapers. Readers want to know about drugs, the effects of chemical additives in foods, new discoveries in medicine, new sources of energy, frontiers in the space program. At the *Post* O'Toole covers the physical sciences and two other reporters write about medical subjects. One covers national stories—health programs and legislation—and the other covers local medical subjects—what is going on in hospitals and medical schools in the Washington area. The two medical reporters share the coverage of advances in medicine, new treatments for disease, new drugs, and other such subjects.

All the science reporters put in long working hours. Eighty hour weeks with no time off are common, O'Toole says. "Without that nothing would get done. You wouldn't have anything in the paper. You try to cover the news. It's not as if anyone's trying to screw you; it's just that the news happens every day."

Some stories for O'Toole are events, such as the manned space launches. "That," says O'Toole, "is like being a sportswriter and covering the World Series. They're events that almost handle themselves. All it takes is a lot of time; that's all."

Other stories require more digging. Occasionally

O'Toole will come across a story while reading a scientific journal. He once wrote a story about a lung disease which is caused by breathing in asbestos. He read about the disease in a medical journal and then interviewed the doctors who had written the article. His interview led to information about another disease caused by breathing in asbestos, which was a cancer of the lining of the lung. So a journal article led him to two good stories.

Even though he rarely comes across such a find as that one, he keeps reading scientific publications. "First of all," he says, "it's good mental exercise. It keeps you in touch with what's going on. It sometimes gives you a lot of other ideas. Also it keeps you in touch with the professionals, scientists. And they like to be called when they have pieces in journals."

The key to being a good science writer, O'Toole emphasizes, is to keep circulating, to keep touching base with people who might be good sources, and to try to stay ahead of the news. The wire services can cover daily events, he says, such as government press conferences, while reporters from papers like the *Post* and the *New York Times* should be looking ahead, trying to discover what is going to be news next week and then writing it today.

He picks up stories from various places. On one occasion he had a conversation with Dr. James Fletcher, the director of the National Aeronautics and Space Administration, at a cocktail party. In the course of this conversation he asked Dr. Fletcher if he knew that there was a stained glass window in the National Cathedral in Washington which depicted the moon with the astronauts' footprints in it.

"Oh, yes," Dr. Fletcher replied. "I know about that. As a matter of fact, they're going to put a moon rock into that window." Then he stopped. "Oh, I shouldn't have told you," he said. "It hasn't been announced yet." The next day on the front page of the Style section there was a feature story by Thomas O'Toole about the gift of the moon rock to the National Cathedral and all the measures which would have to be taken to make the window secure so that the moon rock could not be stolen.

This story dropped on O'Toole out of the blue. He got another story about the same time from bits and pieces which he learned while putting together a long Sunday article on the future of the space program. In the course of a number of interviews with people working at NASA he found that one of the projects being planned was flying a rock or soil sample from the planet Mars back to the earth. One person said that the agency had not decided whether this was a high priority project or not; another said more or less the same thing. Finally he went to talk to Dr. Fletcher, the administrator of the agency, and found out that the project had top priority but that biologists were afraid that there would be contamination in the rocks since there may be life on Mars. Thus consideration was being given to examining the samples in an orbiting space capsule before bringing them back to earth. This story made the front page a few days after O'Toole's interview with Fletcher.

Of course, O'Toole is very pleased when he has an exclusive story which no other paper has gotten. Both the moonrock story and Mars mission story were exclusives; no other paper had them. He got another exclusive story by using a classic reporters' technique—bluffing.

President Nixon's first adviser on energy policy was John Love, formerly governor of Colorado. In February

1974, a lawyer friend of O'Toole's called him up and told him that a rumor was circulating that Love was going to resign and that he would be replaced by William Simon. The lawyer had clients who were closely connected to the oil companies, so O'Toole considered him a reliable source for the story.

O'Toole then called up Simon's office on a Saturday morning and was told that he was in a meeting. So he said to the secretary, "Well, I'd like him to call me back because we're going to break a story that he's been made energy czar and that John Love is on the way out." Twenty minutes later Simon returned the call and confirmed the story.

When Governor George Wallace was shot in Laurel, Maryland, in 1972, the *Post* had the first news that he was paralyzed and the first news that his spinal cord was severed. O'Toole got both those stories. He had a friend who knew a doctor at the hospital where Wallace was being treated. O'Toole called the doctor. For a number of reasons, O'Toole surmised that the doctor was a liberal, and therefore unsympathetic to Wallace's politics.

The doctor was hesitant to reveal any information. O'Toole promised that his name would not be used in a story. He wavered. O'Toole kept pressing. He used the name of his friend who was also a doctor. Finally the doctor agreed. That night he called O'Toole from a pay phone and said that he had seen the x-rays. They did not show definitively that the spinal cord had been cut and more x-rays were being taken. Wallace was paralyzed, however.

O'Toole ran that story in the next morning's paper and reporters from everywhere else were chasing the story all day. That night the doctor called again and said that the second set of x-rays showed that the spinal cord was cut: O'Toole had another exclusive story.

Earlier in his career when O'Toole was a young reporter with the *Wall Street Journal*, he crashed a stockholders meeting of the New York Giants baseball team and broke the story that the team was moving to San Francisco. A stockholder had given him a proxy and he went into a meeting that was closed to the press, using a false name. "I was shaking like a leaf," he recalls. "I lied. But I'd do the same thing over again."

Sometimes, O'Toole confirmed, he gets a story by sheer luck, but then luck is often being in the right place at the right time. He emphasizes that you have to keep circulating and you have to keep talking to people. Then stories keep coming your way.

"You use as many sources as you possibly can," O'Toole says, "juggle as many as you possibly can all at once. Some people liken it to being a whirling dervish." And O'Toole thrives on this kind of pace. He likes running around after sources and he likes being constantly busy.

The *Post* is always in competition with the *New York Times* for good stories and O'Toole is pleased every time he beats a *Times* reporter on a story. But sometimes the *Times* gets one first.

On one occasion O'Toole had a lead on a story about a report on the effects of defoliation in Vietnam. According to his source the report had been prepared for the National Academy of Sciences but publication was being held up by the Department of Defense.

O'Toole made some phone calls and was told several times that the report was not available yet. Then he left for a tour of the atomic energy center at Oak Ridge, Tennessee, after having told the national editor that the defoliation report story would break the following week.

The very next day the story appeared in the *New York*

Times under the byline of John Finney. "He's tough competition," O'Toole says. "He has very good sources on the Senate Foreign Relations Committee and I know damn well that's where he got it. He didn't have the full report either. What he had was probably the bare bones, a summary or something. But he beat us."

O'Toole was called out of a press briefing at Oak Ridge to answer a phone call from one of the editors in Washington asking why the *New York Times* had the story when O'Toole had told them it wouldn't break until the following week. Chagrined, O'Toole had to admit that Finney had beaten him, and another *Post* reporter had to pick up the story quickly to write something for the next day's edition.

"Win a few, lose a few," O'Toole says. "You try to win more than you lose. And we do. A lot more. But you're up against tough competition."

O'Toole sniffs out most of his stories himself, using the many sources he has cultivated during his years as a science reporter. Sometimes editors have story suggestions. On big stories, such as a series of articles on energy done in 1971 before there was much public concern about the shortage of natural resources, editors usually have sound judgment, according to O'Toole. They have a good sense of when a "take out" or summary story should be done. For example, when the Arab oil embargo ended in March 1974, O'Toole was asked to do a take out explaining what the effects had been, how many jobs had been lost, how people had reacted to the shortages, and so on.

On spot news O'Toole is impatient with suggestions that editors make. "Editors hear an awful lot of rumors," he says. "They get stuff phoned in to them by anonymous tipsters. It's usually a waste of time. Of course there's the outside chance that what they come up with is true, so you have to check it out."

He also has his gripes with the copy desk as all reporters do. When the pages are being laid out and there is a shortage of space, the editors usually cut the story at the end. "Very often," says O'Toole, "you write a story with an ending, and you come in the next day and there's no ending to the story. It just hangs there." To avoid this, he must be in the office late at night, when the copy is edited. "And you work hard enough so you don't want to hang around too late at night."

During his years as a science writer O'Toole has learned to interpret complex and difficult material for people who know nothing about science. He has been doing this for so long that it is almost second nature to him now. In fact, in many of his stories he is educating people rather than simply reporting news.

At the end of March 1974, he went to the Jet Propulsion Laboratory in Pasadena, California, to cover the flight of the spacecraft Mariner 10 to within 500 miles of the planet Mercury. This was a historic event because it was the first time that a spacecraft had approached that planet, and the photographs taken from Mariner 10 gave a view of Mercury 100 times better than any telescopic viewing from the earth.

The series of articles which O'Toole wrote about this event were capsule lessons in astronomy. He explained that the photographs showed that Mercury's surface looked something like that of the moon, with deep craters in its surface. He explained that the planet's temperature had been taken from the spacecraft and that it was 600 degrees Farenheit and that Mercury had a thin atmosphere made up of the gases argon and helium. Instruments on Mariner 10 also measured the planet's density and found it to be the heaviest of the planets since it is mostly made up of iron. The articles were written so that a person with no scientific background could easily understand them but they contained a great amount of detail and O'Toole did not write down to his audience.

He believes that science writing should educate people and that every science story should do some teaching. "There ought to be that feeling," he says, "that there is somebody out there, a kid, primarily a sixth grader or seventh grader or a high school kid who just might get turned on by this story so why don't you take a little effort to make it that way. You don't always do it; you're in a hurry half the time. But you should do that."

O'Toole started out as a chemistry major at St. Peter's College, a small Jesuit school in New Jersey. By the time he was a junior he began to realize that a future as a chemist was not for him but he decided to finish as a chemistry major anyway. Meanwhile, he was also writing for the college magazine and wondered if he could combine his chemistry major with writing in some way. When he began to discuss career plans with his faculty advisors, he learned that a recent chemistry graduate of the school had gotten a job at *Business Week* magazine as a science writer.

But he wasn't quite ready to give up the idea of a career in science. After college he was a special student at MIT. "They separate the men from the boys up there," he said wryly, "and I was one of the boys. I quit." Then he went into the army for two years and, after he got out, he earned a master's degree in journalism from Boston University.

His first job was at the *Cape Cod Standard Times* as a general assignment reporter. "I didn't want to do science right away," he said, "although I knew I was interested. I wanted to work at journalism first, find out what the business was like." After six months there he went to the *Asbury Park Press* in New Jersey, lived at home and saved enough money to buy a car.

Then he wrote to the *Wall Street Journal* in New York and was asked to come in for an interview. The *Journal* was interested in his science background and put him to work covering the chemical industry. He began writing about drugs and medicine which he did not particularly enjoy. Finally he was assigned to cover the physical sciences and space. This was around 1960 when the manned space program had just been announced and there was a great deal of excitement about space exploration.

"There was a lot of 'gee whiz' writing in those days," O'Toole says. "People discovered science writing when Sputnik went up in 1957 and there was a good five year period when there was too much gee whiz stuff. Nobody writes a gee whiz story any more. There's more emphasis on interpretation than there was then."

After five years at the *Journal* O'Toole was ready for an opportunity to do something else. He had gotten a good background as a science reporter, had gained a reputation working on a prestigious paper but he wasn't going anywhere. The *Wall Street Journal* has a policy of hiring young reporters with promise and training them well, but there is no upward mobility.

In 1962 O'Toole jumped at the chance of helping to start a monthly news magazine called *USA 1*. It folded after six months. Then he freelanced for a while, wrote a few stories for the *Saturday Evening Post*, but it was about to go under too, so he took a job at *Time* magazine.

At *Time* correspondents report from the field and writers in the New York office transform their reports into the copy which appears in the magazine. O'Toole was a writer handling science, medicine, and business. He never had a chance to report his own story or try out any of his ideas and he felt that he was losing his identity as a writer. "You tend to write the way the magazine wants you to write," he says.

From *Time* he went to the *New York Times* and covered technology for about a year. He was frustrated there too by the bigness of the operation and the layers of bureaucracy. When he had a story suggestion it would sometimes be days before he got a response from an editor, and sometimes he would never get an answer.

When Howard Simons, the *Post*'s science writer, was moved up to managing editor and O'Toole was offered his job he was ready to leave the *Times*. At the *Post* he likes being able to get a quick response from editors if he has something to pursue and he likes having the freedom to move outside his beat from time to time if he comes up with a good story idea.

When Rockefeller was proposed as Vice President by President Ford in 1974, O'Toole was the one who had the idea of looking into his finances. He talked to Howard Simons, the managing editor, and Simons said "O.K. Go ahead and do it." He collaborated on the story with Bill Greider, a political reporter.

"At the *Times* you wouldn't suggest that story," he said, "because you'd know you'd get nowhere and you would certainly have nothing to do with it. Here they're a lot freer and they swing. And we get the stories that way."

O'Toole's working schedule does not leave much time for leisure. When he is not traveling or working late on a story he stays at home with his wife and children. "I don't play golf or anything like that," he says. "I do two things. I work and I stay with the kids."

He is pleased that his oldest son shares some of his

interest in science, since neither his wife nor his other children have a scientific bent. "My oldest son memorized all the parts of the human body when he was six," O'Toole says proudly. "He's fourteen now and he's built his own oscilloscope. He reads every electronics magazine in sight and he knows the ins and outs of a stereo set. He enjoys the fact that his father writes for the paper. He's expressed no great interest in doing it himself yet, although he may."

Social life is difficult for O'Toole. "I don't have any," he says. "My social life is my friends here at the office." Then he reconsidered. "We do go to the theater. We break our backs to do that." He is pleased that Washington is now beginning to come alive and offer some of the same cultural life he enjoyed in New York—theater, dance, art galleries, and good restaurants.

O'Toole's advice for aspiring science reporters is to minor in a science and major in economics or history, not English. He finds that because he did not take enough economics or history, and many of his stories deal with economic issues, he has had to do a lot of reading to keep up.

He doesn't have much use for journalism schools except for the graduate schools at Columbia University and the University of Missouri, because they both have daily newspapers which all the students work on and which give them practical experience. He suggests going to a college which has a daily newspaper and working on the newspaper to gain writing experience.

A good course in typing is also useful, especially since more and more papers are beginning to use electronic equipment which will require reporters to type their copy without strikeovers or misplaced letters.

O'Toole does not see the science field expanding

greatly unless newspapers combine science and energy. Then coverage will expand. Since he writes on energy and the physical sciences, he is very overworked and has been trying for months, in vain, to get the editors to add a fourth reporter to his department. The greatest number of science stories have to do with medicine and the human body. Readers are interested in what may affect them. New discoveries in cancer research or the latest treatment for heart disease are always big stories. Or if a prominent person has a medical problem like Mrs. Ford's breast cancer or ex-President Nixon's phlebitis, people want to know all about it.

In the physical sciences O'Toole thinks that the biggest stories are going to be in astronomy, and these are the stories that interest him most. But aside from energy stories, he finds it hard to convince editors that science is big news. "Editors for some reason are turned off science right now. Everything is Watergate and politics," he says. "There's only one way to get them interested and that's to go out and get a good story." And this is what he tries every day to do—get his science story on page one.

CHAPTER 9

Two Photographers

*J*ust as *Post* reportorial positions are considered plums in the newspaper world, jobs on the *Post* photographic staff are also prized by newspaper photographers. Many want to be hired and few want to leave. Salaries are high; working conditions are good; assignments are varied. Bill Snead, the assistant managing editor for photography and himself a fine photographer, said that during the two years that he had been in charge of the department not one photographer had left.

Matthew Lewis and Frank Johnston are two members of the *Post*'s staff of 20 photographers, in some ways different but both restless, competitive, never satisfied with what they have just done, always thinking they could get that one shot that would be better than the last one.

Matthew Lewis is in his mid-forties, a black man who grew up in McDonald, Pennsylvania, a small town near Pittsburgh, where his grandfather had his own photographic studio. Since his parents were divorced, Lewis was brought up by his grandparents and his aunts and he absorbed knowledge about photography almost in spite of himself. He helped set up lights and other equipment and watched his grandfather mix chemicals; he learned to be a craftsman and a perfectionist. "My grandfather was good," Lewis recalled. "He had to be to be black and make a living in that place because most of his customers were white."

Young Matthew had no desire to become a photographer. He was more interested in music. After he finished high school, he went to Howard University and the University of Pittsburgh and then joined the Navy, without graduating. After several years in the Navy he went to work as a sandblaster in a Pittsburgh foundry. By this time he was married and had children and was working hard to get his promotions in the foundry.

Meanwhile, he began to get interested in photography, not portrait photography, but news photography. Lewis made a darkroom in a shed next to his house and began taking pictures all the time. He managed to be first on the scene at an accident when a train hit a car crossing the railroad tracks and sold it to one of the Pittsburgh papers. While still working full-time in the foundry, Lewis spent most of his spare time taking pictures—baby pictures, wedding pictures, graduation pictures—any assignments which would give him a chance to increase his portfolio and make enough money to replenish his supplies.

After he had been doing photography for several years, his aunts, who were college teachers, suggested that he apply for a job in the audio-visual department of a black college. His wife died; he was going nowhere in the foundry, and finally a job opened up at Morgan State College in Baltimore. So Lewis spent eight years there in a dual capacity—as an audio-visual technician and a photographer. He also set up a studio and freelanced for local newspapers.

Then he began looking for a job as a full-time photographer—anywhere. He was interviewed at news agencies, magazines, newspapers. He met Gordon Parks who was then a staff photographer at *Life* magazine. Lewis was discouraged because he was already over thirty and didn't seem to be getting anywhere but Parks encouraged him and said it was never too late to start. Finally one day Lewis brought his portfolio to the *Washington Post*, was interviewed and hired.

Matthew Lewis had doubts about a career in photography. By the time he had decided what he did want to do it took him a long time to break in and to finally get a job which was professionally satisfying. Frank Johnston, on the other hand, never wanted to be anything but a news photographer. His father was chief photographer for the *Philadelphia Inquirer* and Frank was completely fascinated by what his father did. He first began to work with a camera when he was about six years old. When he was twelve his father gave him a news camera of his own, a four-by-five Speed Graphic.

As a college student at the University of Pennsylvania he helped pay his expenses by freelancing and working as a copy boy for United Press International. Then when he went into the Army after college he landed an assignment on the company newspaper taking pictures. After his military service he wanted a job with the UPI. He wrote letter after letter asking for work and finally his persistence paid off. He was called to New York for an interview and hired. Later one of the editors who hired him told him: "I can remember this young kid from Philadelphia. I'd get a letter at least once a week asking me for a job. We had no choice but to hire you. We got tired of hearing from you."

Frank Johnston's first assignment when he was hired in 1963 was Austin, Texas. When President Kennedy came to Texas in November, Johnston waited in Austin to cover a big Democratic dinner which was to take place there after the President's visit to Dallas. He walked into the wire room about five minutes to twelve on November 22 and heard three bells ring on the news wire and saw the first dispatches come in over the wire announcing that the President had been shot.

Johnston was sent to Dallas in the Texas Rangers' private plane and covered the aftermath of the assassination. He was standing in the basement of the Dallas jail when Jack Ruby stepped out of the crowd and shot Lee Harvey Oswald. All the cameramen of course reached out with their cameras. Bob Jackson of the *Dallas Times Herald* leaned in front of Frank Johnston's camera and blocked part of the frame. He took the shot of Oswald clutching his stomach that won a Pulitzer Prize and Johnston got only the bottom half of Oswald's body. But he did get all the rest of the shots—the police tackling Ruby on the floor and grabbing the gun out of his hand.

After a coup like that Johnston was off to a good start. He was soon promoted to bureau manager and ran the Philadelphia picture bureau for about a year. But Frank Johnston is not a man who is happy sitting behind a desk for very long. He got tired of shuffling papers and volunteered for an assignment in Vietnam. While he was waiting, he was sent to the Dominican Republic to cover the revolution there. He then spent 14 months in Vietnam and in 1968 came back to an assignment in New York where he covered the student uprising at Columbia University and the political campaigns. Then in September of that year he came to the *Post*.

Johnston is a news photographer all the way, an action man, used to competing with the Associated Press to beat them on deadlines, attuned to the kind of split-second timing required to be in exactly the right place at the right time to get that once in a lifetime shot. Lewis is also an excellent news photographer but he seems to be moving in a different direction. He is reflective and becoming more interested in magazine photography and even in portrait photography like his grandfather. And this surprises him. He never thought he would want to be a portrait photographer.

For about a year Lewis has been assigned full time to work for Potomac, the *Post*'s Sunday magazine. He likes this assignment because he has a chance to work in color and to cover a variety of subjects. Before he came to the Post he had been interested in assignments with *Look* or *Life* but, by the time he had a portfolio ready, *Look* was on its last leg and *Life* was not in very good shape either.

Lewis had found, after nine years of news photography, covering the Redskins football team, the Apollo 9 shot, the demonstrations at the Democratic convention in 1968, that news photography was growing stale for him. The 1960s, especially the latter years of the decade, were years when news was breaking fast, dramatic events followed each other in rapid succession, fashions, customs, and habits were changing, and there was always something to photograph. Lewis could feel things beginning to slow down on the news side during the 1970s, so he found the magazine assignment a welcome change, a chance to grow and develop and learn something new.

In magazine photography, Lewis says, one impression that people have is that you have a lot more time than in news photography. This is not always so, he points out, recalling that he was given an assignment to come up with a cover photo on medical laboratories in the District of Columbia in less than two hours. On other occasions he can work more slowly. When he did a story on Elvin Hayes, of the Washington Capital Bullets basketball team, he went to the stadium three times, experimented with different shutter speeds and lens openings, and photographed his subject playing in different games.

Sometimes he has to work under real pressure such as when he went to the White House to photograph President Nixon's press secretary, Ronald Ziegler. The lights were turned on and he was given about a minute to get his picture. "We wanted to shoot both black and white and color and I never had the opportunity. I couldn't take the chance; I couldn't waste the time using black and white because it took three weeks to get that particular date."

On other occasions he has had to photograph people who do not like to be photographed. One such person is the elderly writer Katherine Anne Porter. Lewis went to that assignment knowing that she was nervous about having her picture taken and trying to figure out how to overcome her fear. As it turned out she relaxed very quickly and he spent two hours with her, taking pictures, talking, and listening to records. He felt pleased that he was able to establish rapport with her so quickly.

Lewis is a reserved man, somewhat shy, very thoughtful, not at all pushy. He finds it difficult to photograph someone who does not want to be photographed because he is sensitive to the person's feelings and does not want to intrude. When he has an assignment like that, he just takes the picture as fast as he can and then leaves.

Lewis explains that the essence of magazine photography is illustrating, figuring out what picture will have the greatest impact in combination with the text. In the process of getting that photograph he has to make dozens of very fast decisions—from what angle to photograph the subject, what kind of lighting to use, what shutter speed and lens opening, what distance, always keeping in mind what the story says and how the photograph will relate to the written word.

Lewis is sitting on a desk top in the photographic studio in the basement of the *Post* building waiting for someone who is supposed to appear to have her picture taken. She never comes. He strokes his greying hair and looks thoughtful when asked what kind of photography he would really like to do. He pauses for a few minutes.

"I can tell you what I don't like," he says. "I don't like covering receptions, and parties, and luncheons. It's too repetitive. You take the same shot over and over again."

His favorite assignments are sports and fashion: sports because the fast action poses such a challenge to a photographer and fashion because he likes working in color and he has not done enough of this kind of photography to be satisfied that he has mastered it.

Lewis now feels that he is going through a transition as a photographer. For a while he felt that news photography was what interested him the most. Now he finds that he is turned on by advertising photography and fashion photography in magazines such as *Vogue* and *Harper's Bazaar*.

He likes being busy, coming in to the office in the morning, and being sent out on assignments that keep him occupied all day. He doesn't like sitting around at a desk waiting for something to do. And photography is his life. There are no vacations. "I begin to get uneasy after two days when I haven't shot any pictures," he says.

Lewis lives alone in Silver Spring, Maryland, just outside of Washington. He is separated from his second wife who lives in Miami with their fifteen-year-old son. Lewis is pleased that his son is showing an interest in photography. He shot some photographs of Sammy Davis, Jr., which were published in a local black newspaper.

Lewis has been given a specialized assignment on
Potomac which is supposed to be rotated periodically
among members of the staff to give staff members a
change of pace. Frank Johnston is a general assignment
photographer. All the general assignment photographers have rotating work schedules. One week a person
may work from ten in the morning until six in the
evening. Another week it will be twelve to eight. The
next it may be four in the afternoon to midnight.

Johnston doesn't mind this schedule although he says
that some weeks he hardly sees his wife at all, since she
is a public school teacher and goes to work every
morning at eight o'clock.

When he first came to the *Post*, Johnston was
assigned full time to the White House. He found this an
interesting assignment although, as with White House
reporters, a lot of time is spent sitting in the press room
waiting for something to happen. Then there will be an
announcement that a picture session will take place.
Ten or fifteen photographers and four or five television
cameramen file into the President's office and are given
thirty seconds to a minute to take their pictures. The
experienced photographers know how to head quickly
for the best positions in the room but the novices can be
squeezed out completely. If a photographer fails to get a
good shot, the photography editor selects a wire service
picture instead.

Johnston has a sense of humor and once in a while,
while covering the White House, he had a chance to use
it. Soon after President Nixon's inauguration in January
1969 the photographers were invited in for a session to
take pictures of the First Family's two dogs. Johnston
got a shot of three photographers, two from AP and one
from UPI, squatting with their cameras cocked, while
the two dogs grinned photogenically into Johnston's

camera. His photo was prominently displayed on the front page of the Style section.

After two years at the White House Johnston was ready for a little more variety and asked to be put on general assignment. He has covered streakers on the University of Maryland campus, rock concerts, demonstrations and riots where he has had to dodge bottles and bricks, and special features where he has been able to work at a slightly slower pace than he does on breaking news stories.

He likes having the opportunity at the *Post* to do feature and semi-documentary work, which he didn't have a chance to do at the wire service. When Ron Kessler wrote his seven-part investigative series on the Postal Service, Johnston was assigned to take the pictures to go with it. He spent several days around various post offices taking pictures of people working at different jobs. That was an assignment he enjoyed.

Most of his assignments are near enough to Washington so that he can come back to the *Post* darkroom to develop and print his pictures but sometimes he is too far away to get back the same day. In such cases he takes portable darkroom equipment and a portable transmitter with him. He develops and prints his pictures in his hotel room, connects the transmitter to the telephone, and sends a print back through the transmitter.

The transmitter is about the size of a portable typewriter with an eight by ten inch drum. A photoelectric cell scans the drum and the black and white of the photograph are changed to sound waves, transmitted through the telephone and changed back to black and white tones by a receiver in the *Post* building. The receiver turns out a black and white glossy print with a caption about ten minutes after the transmission begins.

Frank Johnston foresees further technological advances—for instance, video cameras which would eliminate the need to process film.

Now a photographer usually has to carry several cameras, as well as flash equipment, extra film, different lenses, and a walkie-talkie so that he can keep in touch with the office. Most of the photographers use company cars with two-way radios installed in them but Frank Johnston and several other staff photographers have their own motorcycles which they sometimes use for assignments. "We're the Easy Riders of the *Washington Post*," Johnston says. "We use our bikes because they're easy to park and easy to get around town. If you have a nice day you can't resist." In his jeans, boots, turtleneck sweater, and aviator glasses Johnston looks ready for action on his bike. All he needs is a black leather jacket.

There are only twenty photographers on the staff and nearly three hundred writers and editors. That's a ratio of one picture person for every twenty word people. So it is very clear that pictures are subordinate to words. Even so, the *Post* displays photographs prominently. The front page usually has two or three photos. The first page of the Metro section uses photos generously and the Style section uses imaginative layouts with well displayed pictures. In addition, there are occasionally special sections where photographs are important.

Nevertheless, there is always tension between the word people and the visual people. As the paper gets bigger and the number of word people increases, they will inevitably make more demands for space. Frank Johnston thinks he can see this trend developing since he has been at the *Post*—fewer pictures, more words, and more crowded page layouts to make space for longer stories.

As Matthew Lewis said, a news photographer is an

illustrator. The picture helps to tell a reporter's story. The photographer may be covering an event where the story itself determines what the picture will be, or there may be a story where the photographer has to think up a picture which will convey the meaning of a story at a glance.

For artistic photographers who like to shoot clouds, snow storms, birds, and animals, there are some opportunities in newspaper work. The *Post* occasionally publishes such "stand alone" art, both by its own staff members and by freelancers, but the basic job is reporting with the camera, being quick, having a nose for news, and being on the spot to get the story.

CHAPTER 10

"A Matter of Opinion"

"I worked as a DJ for a station in Dover, Delaware—
for about a year and a half, you know, rip and read and
do the whole thing," said Bob Asher in a mellow voice.
A native of Washington, Asher did a six-month hitch in
the Air Force and then looked for another job in radio,
preferably in the Capitol area. The "something to do
while waiting for a radio job" was to answer an ad for
copyboy at the *Post*. He got the job. That was more
than fifteen years ago. Asher is now a *Post* editorial
writer specializing in metropolitan issues.

When asked "Where did you go after copyboy?"
Asher shoots back what should have been obvious:
"Head copyboy!" He adds, "Being head copyboy was
the hardest job I've ever had—trying to keep everyone
happy. You know, aspirin for the secretaries, getting
coffee, running proof." Taking dictation from reporters
taught Asher a lot about writing style and the reporter's
job.

In those days the *Post* had two-paragraph summaries
of church sermons in the back of the paper. This was
Asher's assignment, and he thinks that during his ten
months as copyboy he visited dozens of churches. In
addition, he was given night assignments. After running
about all day, he was told to go to the library for
background information and then cover the Arlington
County Zoning Board Hearings, or some such.

Asher's first byline came with a story about a writer
on animals at the National Zoo. He had a staff

photographer with him and he treated it like a feature story. It was thrilling to see his name on the piece but he admits today that it wasn't half as difficult to write as a short police piece with fifteen pounds of information about a traffic accident that had to be squeezed into three paragraphs.

In the years between copyboy and editorial writer Asher did a variety of jobs in the newsroom. He bounced from the local beat and general assignment to reporting from Capitol Hill and City Hall. As picture editor he wrote photograph captions and learned the business of production. He was day city editor, night state editor, and copydesk editor.

In 1969 Asher spent a year at Columbia University studying advanced international reporting on a Ford Foundation fellowship. After this hiatus, Asher was not anxious to return to his old job. He wanted something different. He had heard that most of the editorial staff members enjoyed their jobs, and he was impressed with the few editorial meetings he had attended. So when the local affairs man on the editorial staff left, Asher asked for his job. The talks he had with Philip Geyelin, the editorial page editor, and his assistant Meg Greenfield were very casual. When they were satisfied that he would be a good choice for the position, Asher had a chat with Katharine Graham. It wasn't a quiz of Asher's views on political issues but rather a chance to get to know each other.

"I guess the chemistry, budget, tide and time all clicked and I was there. We decided to try each other for six months. I've been here four years now—doesn't seem that long. It's like just the other day," says Asher.

In bouncing from one job to another in the news-room, Asher had learned to shift gears easily, but his assignment to the editorial staff was the most radical change he had made in his career. While the newsroom is loud, frenzied, and hustling, the editorial department seems always calm and conducive to contemplation. Asher's initial impression of the editorial staff was a very conservative bunch of men, who were pensive and seemingly isolated.

Though every job has a routine, Asher's day is more varied than most. Usually there is a morning meeting of the editorial staff at ten, presided over by Geyelin. The meeting is free-wheeling and varies in length. Ideas are thrown out for discussion and though Asher's province is the metropolitan area, he says, "If I felt particularly moved to scream about something like Watergate or the President or the Middle East, I would do so."

The political viewpoints of the staff members are varied. There are no "extremists" but their debates are indeed rousing. Asher says, "We try not to fall into a political philosophy that would be predictable. People try to force us into one. If you ask them today how we came out on the Carswell and Haynsworth nominations, they would probably say we opposed them both. This is not so. We said Haynsworth should be confirmed. This was after a complicated discussion. It was taken on the merits only after one of us who used to cover the Supreme Court presented the case for Haynsworth as a lawyer and judge and not the politics that goes along with it."

A problem for the editorial board is how to change from a previously taken position like the attitude toward the Vietnam War. Asher feels that this has to be done very carefully. There has to be continuity in editorial policy. "If you want to make a 180° turn in position, you have to be careful to figure how to get there semantically as well as logically," he cautions.

Katharine Graham is very interested in the editorial

policy of her newspaper. She attends editorial conferences frequently, but Asher has never detected any
pressure from her. The staff does not get orders from the
publisher on editorial policy. She has put her trust in her
editorial page editor and his team, and feels they should
decide the policy on their own. "I guess," said Asher
wistfully, "if your batting averages were off constantly
you'd change the team."

At the *Post* the editorial staff is not concerned in any
way with fiscal matters. When asked about it Asher
replies, "That's her worry. She has a whole distinguished staff of corporate people who do that and that's
fine. It's a credit to the paper. The two things have to be
divorced. We would certainly acknowledge that while
people might rant and rail about big business, a large,
financially healthy newspaper has so much more freedom—don't have to worry if someone threatens with
yanking their advertising."

After the editorial board meeting, the remainder of
Asher's morning is spent making appointments, calling
contacts, and researching background for editorial
pieces. Lunches, either at the *Post* or with guests
outside, are usually a combination of business and a
break. Asher usually spends afternoons writing, but he
does not write an editorial every day. He likes his job
because it gives him time to study complicated issues.

By five o'clock in the afternoon the editorials start
coming into Phil Geyelin's office. He and Meg Greenfield will select a combination of editorials and the
order in which they will appear the next day. Not all
editorials are run the day they are written. The editorial
staff's production team begins the puzzle of fitting them
into the left side of the page as well as laying out the rest
of the sheet and the Op-Ed page, which consists of
signed columns by staff members, syndicated writers,

and guest columnists, and also letters to the editor. Then, if there is time, Asher will begin writing a new piece and work on it till the end of the day, about seven-thirty.

Friday is always busy. No one likes work on weekends, but editorials have to be written for Saturday, Sunday, and Monday. So on Friday afternoon everyone rushes to finish three or four editorials and then "dumps them on poor Phil's desk at seven o'clock."

The style of writing in editorials has to be consistent. It is the job of the editor to see that the level of taste and style is even. It is, however, a great game among Asher's friends to guess who wrote what editorial. Asher confesses that some of them get quite good at it, despite Phil Geyelin's best efforts.

While most reporters are looking for their bylines, the editorial writers are always anonymous. They are the voice of the editorial policy. The "we" of the editorial page is quite different from the more personal "we" of the columnist. However, a longer, more complex and personal analysis of an issue may be written by an editorial staff member, and, if it's accepted, it would appear on the right hand side of the page with a byline.

Asher never attended a school of journalism. He had on-the-job training. His fellowship year at Columbia was more concentrated on foreign affairs and policy than on the craft of journalism. For him that year "was a great taste of mid-career university life." He now teaches a course in journalism, but worries that the schools get too involved with the "carpentry" of the craft. He feels that other skills such as science, political science, and an understanding of fiscal matters are far more important than the mechanics of putting together a newspaper. That skill can be learned by doing.

The usual political differences of the liberal news staff

and the more moderate editorial writers concerns Asher. He feels the problem is partly "age and ideological isolation." The news people are out in the field every day. Asher tries to get out as often as possible. He keeps in contact with the people who are making the news. "If you don't," he says, "you get too attached to old friends and old impressions. Let's face it, city hall in '67 is not city hall in '74."

An important way for Asher to keep in touch with the community problems is as a private citizen. He and his wife try to get out, keep their ears open, attend public functions, and listen to speeches of candidates as well as complaints of neighbors. Their children attend public schools, so they are intimately aware of one of the city's major concerns.

An area of experience that has kept Asher in touch with the problems of the working people has been his union activities. Since 1964 he has been involved in the business of the Newspaper Guild, which is the union that represents the news, editorial, clerical and business staff on the paper. He was asked to be unit chairman, to represent the Post employees in contract negotiations with the management of the paper.

"I didn't know anything," Asher said, "but I was willing to learn, and it was a learning experience."

He was unit chairman for a couple of years and then he was asked to run for president of the Washington-Baltimore local, which represents the employees of all the papers in those two cities. He ran and won and served as president of the local for two years. Then his union participation subsided.

Early in 1974 he was asked to be on a twenty-person committee which was negotiating with management for a new contract. Asher was reluctant to participate because he had had enough of all-night and weekend negotiating sessions but he was finally persuaded to join the committee.

"It was rewarding," he said, "because I got to know what was going on in the rest of the building. I was working with people in accounting, circulation, advertising and other departments and that was a good experience."

There was no lack of all night meetings. The old contract expired on March 31, 1974, and a new contract had not been agreed upon. On April 8, negotiations broke down and the guild employees went on strike. For a few days they were enthusiastic about the strike. Then doubts and fears began to set in and Asher found himself deluged with phone calls from people wanting to know how the negotiations were going, what was being decided, what management representatives were saying. Pressure began to mount from both sides to end the strike and get back to work.

The main issues were financial—a salary increase and the replacement of the *Post*'s profit-sharing plan with a pension plan for employees who were retiring. Finally on April 25 the union members voted to go back to work with a six percent salary increase plus a cost of living increase to be added on at the end of a year and a pension plan, the details of which would be worked out by management and the union.

Though the news and editorial departments are totally independent, the newsroom is a prime source for editorial material. Asher likes to bounce his impressions off the reporters. He says, "I don't expect to have their opinions guide mine, but the impressions of reporters are a factor that should be weighed. They shouldn't be overriding; that would be dangerous, but it's worth getting their views as much as it is of the principal players. Two sides of the story are fine; a third, supposedly objective, side is very useful."

The people in the newsroom are particularly helpful in checking on the accuracy of a piece. In editorial writing, Asher says, "You can't afford inaccuracies especially since it erodes your power of persuasion, and that's our business."

Persuasion is the name of the game but it's difficult to gauge the effectiveness of any one editorial. The reputation of the *Post* is such that people do pay attention, and the editorials are read by the influential members of Congress, the diplomatic community, and the executive branch.

There is one man on the editorial staff, however, who has been particularly dramatic in his effect. During the Army-McCarthy hearings, McCarthy would shave with brush and lather at lunch time "because of that son of a bitch at the *Post*," while Vice President Nixon canceled home delivery of the *Post* because of pressure from his family. The political cartoons of Herblock were the cause.

Squirrelled away in an office that is completely hidden from view, Herbert L. Block turns out five political cartoons a week. Photographs, books, magazines, old Sears Roebuck catalogues, stacks of newspapers, and rows of overstuffed file cabinets are everywhere. His desk and drawing table are cluttered with papers, rough sketches, idea notes, and the usual paraphernalia of a working graphic artist. A deep, soft sofa and blanket show evidence of much use. The room is as relaxed as its occupant.

While attending Lake Forest College, Herblock drew political cartoons for suburban Chicago papers. He did stints with the *Chicago Daily News* and the Scripps-

Howard chain. It was just after World War II that Herblock was invited to work for the *Post* by Eugene Meyer. Meyer sent Herblock a three-month subscription of the *Post* to convince him to join the staff.

"With a cartoon you're basically trying to say something, not just amuse," says Herblock. He tries to do this by keeping his independence. He has his own personal news sources and being close to Washington sources can be a great advantage. Herblock doesn't attend editorial conferences, but he may send a sketch to the editorial page editor just to let him know what's happening.

Political cartoons depend upon the day's events. Herblock is a deadline pusher and some days the news gives him trouble. "You can turn on the radio at six o'clock and find out about some very important event," he said sadly, "and have to throw out all that I've done for the day." Other cartoons have to be held back because a planned summit meeting was rescheduled or a major character was ill. Herblock's office doesn't have the heightened urgency of the newsroom but he is pressured by his need for accuracy and his moral determination.

Herblock has an eight o'clock deadline. The drawing itself takes him a couple of hours to complete. It is syndicated through Field Newspaper Syndicate and prints are mailed to over two hundred newspapers throughout the country and abroad. It usually appears a day or two later in those papers.

Herblock has been in the political cartooning game a long time and has seen many styles come and go. They have ranged from the stock Uncle Sam standing perplexed at the crossroads to the more recent sophisticated European mode. Influenced by the great Thomas

Nast, Boss Tweed's gadfly, Herblock depends more on wit and keen political insight than on graphic style.

The use of symbols is particularly important to the cartoonist's trade. The more personal and inventive the symbol, the better the artist. Herblock is a master of this kind of invention. The Joe McCarthy five o'clock shadow and the Nixon smear paint brush are surely among the best. One obvious symbol caused considerable consternation overseas. When Herblock first used the Capitol dome as background for one of his cartoons, his British audience wanted to know why St. Paul's was in the picture.

It is quite reasonable that both Asher and Herblock should find their way onto the *Post*'s editorial page. They are both bright, inventive, and most of all, enjoy the freedom their jobs allow.

CHAPTER 11

The Evolution of Style

One of the most popular sections of the *Washington Post* is Style, subtitled People/The Arts/Leisure. In the Style section you may find a book review by a prominent guest writer, a humorous column by Art Buchwald, a feature on San Francisco by the West Coast correspondent, a report on a party attended by a number of prominent political figures, an advice column by Ann Landers, a "life-style" portrait of a Cabinet appointee, a preview of a television program, an analysis of changing family values, and a crossword puzzle.

Style's chief creators were executive editor Bradlee and David Laventhol, who became its first editor. In 1968 Bradlee began turning his attention to the women's section, which, under its long-time editor Marie Sauer, was like a little newspaper within a newspaper. The women's section reporters covered parties, fashion, the wives of prominent men, anything that had to do with women. They did page layouts, wrote headlines and photo captions, and supervised production. Since a good number of the editors and reporters were women, this was an excellent training ground for women. Some who started here, like Mary Russell, have gone on to become political reporters and others have found niches in Style.

In the old days, as one reporter recalls, "the women's section was separate but unequal. The editor had to fight to get a photographer for a story or to get anyone in the composing room to pay attention to what we wanted done. Then as soon as it became Style and had men editors, they could get anything they wanted."

The metamorphosis of the women's section was gradual. There were discussions and meetings and gradually the concept of Style emerged—it was to be "devoted to the way Washingtonians live—in the suburbs as well as the city, men and women, white and black, decisionmakers and homemakers," according to the announcement preceding its birth on January 6, 1969.

Not only was Style incorporating the old women's section; it was also taking in the drama and music critics and broadening their mandate to include not just reviews of individual performances, but also a look at the state of the arts—the performers, the theaters and concert halls, the patrons of the arts. Style was planning to take off from the old coverage and go beyond it: in fashion to look, not just at the Paris openings, but at "the way we furnish our lives"; in society, to "reach beyond the party goers and status symbols for insights into 'society' at all levels."

The first issue was a departure from tradition with open page layouts and a lot of photographs. (Laventhol was very strong on graphics.) Articles included a piece on new fashions, Levis and pants, and an article about the parties at President Nixon's inaugural, a traditional story but with a few wry twists, such as the observation that LBJ plates were available at People's Drugstore for $2.00 apiece but that the Nixon chinaware hadn't arrived yet. There was a column of political commentary by Nicholas Von Hoffman, a profile of Mrs. Nixon's social secretary, and a feature on death and life in a West Virginia coal mining town.

Style had many growing pains. Laventhol was offered a job as editor of *Newsday*, the Long Island newspaper, which, of course, he did not refuse. His departure left Style struggling to find an identity under a succession of editors, who found it extremely difficult to manage all the diverse personalities and areas under their jurisdiction. The situation has stabilized somewhat under the present editor Tom Kendrick and his managing editor Lon Tuck, who seem to be able to combine administrative skill, sensitivity, and imagination, a combination which seems essential in coping with such diverse areas as architecture and rock music. They also must deal with such personalities as Richard Coe, veteran drama critic, and Maxine Cheshire, whose sleuthing for her column, Very Important People, often turns up information which proves to be embarrassing for the rich and powerful of Washington. Style has made an effort to link style and substance through development of the "life style," and in exploring trends and changing mores, often using New Journalism techniques.

Style's most prominent columnists, Buchwald, Von Hoffman, and Cheshire, are syndicated. This means that they have made an agreement with an organization called a syndicate that the syndicate will try to sell their columns to as many other newpapers as possible. This arrangement works to everyone's benefit. The *Post* gains prestige when its columnists are widely read in newspapers around the country and the syndicate and the columnist both make money. The opportunity for columnists to earn extra money through syndication also means that the *Post* can keep some of its top writers, who might otherwise be lured away by the offer of higher salaries elsewhere.

There are also a number of syndicated features appearing in Style, which do not originate at the *Post*. Advice and health information columns are very popular. Style carries a nationally syndicated medical question and answer column, and Ann Landers, who is really Eppie Lederer, working out of the *Chicago Sun-Times* and syndicated by Field Enterprises.

These columns do not quite fit in with the urbane, sophisticated tone of the *Post*'s Style writers but they certainly help to fulfill Style's mandate of looking for "insights into 'society' at all levels," and besides they are very popular. There would undoubtedly be protests from readers if these syndicated features were removed from the paper.

All the changes that Style has been through have taken their toll on people involved. Editors and writers have left or been fired and those who remained have had to work under a succession of editors and cope with a highly charged atmosphere and sometimes frenetic work pace.

One of the people who has lived through all these changes is Judith Martin who began her career at the *Post* as a copygirl in the old For and About Women section. She managed, through an old high school friend who was a copyboy, to get an introduction and be interviewed for a job. She was sure she wouldn't be hired because she had never worked on a high school or college paper nor had she ever considered a career on a newspaper. In spite of her failings she was hired for a summer job between her junior and senior years at Wellesley, and she found that she loved working on the paper, in spite of the late night hours and the low pay and being at the absolute bottom level where she took orders from everybody.

In fact, she liked the job so much that she came back to work during Thanksgiving and Christmas vacations, and settled in for good after graduation. She also got married. In those days, the late '50s, having a career was not what most college girls wanted. The thing to do was to marry as soon as possible and produce three or four children. Judith Martin was engaged while she was in college but, instead of flaunting her diamond, she hid her ring in a bureau drawer until after graduation and she told her fiancé Robert that when he got his medical degree she did not intend to pick up and leave her job to follow him around the country if he wanted to change his job.

Robert went to work at the National Institutes of Health outside Washington and the Martins eventually bought a big old house near the National Zoo where they live with their two children.

After a year as copygirl, sharpening pencils, running errands and answering the telephone, Judith Martin became a reporter, "doing the first-year-reporter miserable stories, interviewing secretaries and writing cute little features for Halloween." She soon asked for the diplomatic beat and started out by covering a minor social event while a more experienced reporter went to the main reception of the evening. Eventually Martin became the main reporter of diplomatic social life and also wrote a Sunday column containing tidbits of diplomatic news.

The general rule was that any news which was made at a party or at a press gathering for women reporters was the property of the women's department so that when Senator Fulbright charged that the United States was running the Vietnam pacification program for its own political ends, the news appeared on the women's page because Fulbright was speaking to a group of women reporters.

Most of what Martin reported was pretty frothy—an ambassador arriving, a first secretary being transferred, who was seen at which party, but she also wrote more significant items when she could, such as the problem of racial discrimination which African diplomats faced in trying to find housing or the travel restrictions imposed upon the envoys from Eastern Europe.

In those days Judith Martin's working day began about two in the afternoon and ended around ten-thirty. She spent the afternoons on the telephone following up tips that might lead to a story and in the evening she went to parties, circulating about and talking to as many people as she could. Then she hopped into a taxi, jotting down notes for a story which had to be ready for the ten-thirty deadline.

The Martins organized their lives around Judith's working hours. Since Robert was doing research in a laboratory, he could come and go as he pleased so he kept afternoon and evening work hours too. When their son Nicholas was born, he went onto the same schedule. They arranged their social life with night people, actors and others who weren't on a nine to five routine, and gave dinner parties which started at eleven o'clock.

Both the Martins enjoyed the night working hours but the cocktail circuit was something else. As a result of going to all those diplomatic receptions, Judy says, "I never go to parties. I don't go to anything where I can't sit down. If someone will feed me dinner, O.K." And she has developed a permanent distaste for deviled eggs, tiny open face sandwiches, one-inch square pizzas, and other cocktail party fare.

For about a year before the creation of Style, Martin was working as a general assignment reporter. She handled a variety of assignments, including the White House. Once after a White House party Lyndon Johnson invited her, along with some other women reporters, to the family quarters where he regaled them for hours with all kinds of information. It was a reporter's dream but, before they left, he made the whole conversation off the record. When President Nixon's daughter Julie was married, reporters were barred from the ceremony and the reception but Judy Martin and a colleague, appropriately dressed in pastel gowns with matching grosgrain ribbons in their hair, slipped into the reception by cornering one of the bridesmaids in the ladies' room and following her into the ballroom. As a result of this incident Martin was *persona non grata* at the White House as long as the Nixons were there.

By this time Judy Martin was very tired of women's department reporting. "I had been years and years covering the same parties," she said, "and there's only so much you can squeeze out of it. And then I had faced for years and years people saying, 'Oh, you work for the women's section. I never read the women's section.' And then you found that, sure, they read it because there was a lot of good stuff in there. But the title put everybody off."

As Style began to come off the drawing boards she was anticipating with great delight the changes that the new department would bring. The managing editor was developing mockups of stories and page layouts and Martin would sit with him going over them, long after her working hours were finished. She felt that all the restrictions which she had been working under for so many years would be lifted when the new department got started, and she hasn't been disappointed. She still thinks that she couldn't be working in a better place.

Style has given her the chance to explore many different writing techniques and a variety of subjects. She has written numerous movie reviews, essays, interviews and short features. She is still a general assignment reporter but now has much more freedom.

She is free to explore subjects that interest her and come up with story ideas, and the editors at Style are open to new ideas. For example, on the sixteenth anniversary of the creation of the Barbie doll, she had the idea of writing a satire in the form of an interview with Barbie—about her life style, friends, clothes and so on. The editors thought this was a marvelous idea, sent for the dolls, and discussed the graphics for the story.

"If I have any beat, it's the short bright," she observed. "We've got so many marvelous people who do great in-depth things. So I'm going to be the expert on in-shallow things. People like to read something eight inches in the paper and that's the way I just naturally think."

She also has an outlet for her observations about the little things that bug us all in a Sunday column which is called "Pastiche." In it she has made wry observations on such subjects as the problems of dialing the telephone and getting through to someone in a government agency, and of nostalgia fads and what we should be saving now for the 1970s nostalgia buffs of the 1990s.

Judith Martin is interested in the small details which illuminate an era or which bring to life a personality, what newspaper people call sociology, but what is more precisely the turn of mind of a satirist or a novelist.

She notices what people wear and what they say; she remembers jokes and witty remarks and is quick with her own as well. She remembers that during the 1950s intellectuals considered not owning a television set a mark of status. She is interested in the popularity of the Barbie doll as a sociological phenomenon and in the way Walt Disney films influenced the perception of a whole generation of children.

"You know those Disney images," she says. "Sadness is one big crystal tear and it slides slowly down and falls with a little plop. And evil is unkempt dark hair and red fingernails."

Martin is acutely aware of the small details which make up the style of a person. For example, she once noticed at a White House party that Lyndon Johnson took strawberry tarts one by one from a silver platter, ate the strawberries and returned the tarts to the platter. That detail explained a lot to her about LBJ.

Her own style is distinctive. Ever since college she has worn her hair pulled back into a slightly untidy chignon and, long before they became fashionable, she began wearing gold-rimmed half-moon glasses for reading. Most of the white and blue formica desks in the Style section are more or less bare or else cluttered with stacks of papers but Judith Martin's reflects her own personality. It is neatly arranged with a pottery jug to hold pencils, a row of books in book ends, a white quill pen in a blue glass bottle, fresh flowers in a small vase, an oval mirror in a blue enamel frame and a gold-framed photograph of her husband.

After more than a decade of newspaper writing, she has turned her hand to writing a novel and takes off one day a week to work on her book. "That's enough time," she says. "A lot of it is being written in my head."

Style has provided an outlet for Judith Martin's talents, which would be stifled in a conventional news department where the form of news gathering and writing is more rigid. She is very happy to be where she is.

CHAPTER 12

Writing About the Arts

The Style section pulled together a diverse group of people and a number of areas which had formerly been specialized. Judith Martin came in via the women's section. Another former area of concentration which was brought into Style was culture, what had traditionally been criticism—theater, art, classical music, books, and movies.

In the old days, before Style, the critic would attend a performance or read a book and then write a piece about it. Style writers sometimes follow this format too but they do a great deal more. Instead of reviewing one performance in isolation, they often write essays linking a number of performances or citing trends. The non-specialized critic has also come in with Style. Writers are encouraged to develop familiarity with a number of areas and the areas which are covered have expanded. Not only symphony orchestras but jazz, soul, rock, country and western, and other types of music are covered. Television programs are previewed; performers are interviewed; institutions are examined; the relationship between government and the arts is explored.

Two people who have lived through some of these changes are William McPherson, the editor of Book World and Alan Kriegsman, a versatile critic.

Kriegsman started out as a musicologist at Columbia University in New York but he had dreamed of being a newspaper music critic ever since he met a distant cousin who is a music critic for the *San Francisco*

Examiner. Kriegsman, who was on leave from MIT, serving in the army at the time, asked his cousin how he should go about preparing for a career as a music critic. The answer was, "If it's going to happen at all, it's going to be pure luck. There's nothing you can do to prepare."

After getting out of the Army, Kriegsman went back to New York and enrolled at Columbia, having decided to specialize in music rather than science. Paul Henry Lang, who was chairman of the music department at Columbia at that time, was also music critic for the *New York Herald Tribune* and knew about job openings for music critics. Many of his students would have been interested in these jobs but it never seemed to occur to him to recommend any of them. Kriegsman, who by this time was a graduate student and a member of the faculty, heard Lang talking to someone about an opening for a music critic's job on the *San Diego Union*. As soon as Lang had hung up the phone, Kriegsman walked into his office. Then it suddenly occurred to Lang that Kriegsman might be interested in the job.

Kriegsman applied and was hired but before he went out to San Diego he had to learn how to type. When he arrived in San Diego in 1960, the arts were beginning to flourish. The symphony was making great strides. Ballet and opera companies were formed and many theater groups got started. Kriegsman enjoyed all of these as a private citizen and had a chance to write about many of them as a critic. It was in San Diego that he began to expand from writing solely about music into what he calls "ambidexterous criticism", writing about ballet, opera, musical comedy, and developing expertise in all these areas.

After five years in San Diego and one year in New York as assistant to the president of the Juilliard School of Music, he came to the *Post* in 1966 as a music critic but with the understanding that when the opportunity arose, he would expand into other areas. Style has given him that opportunity. He writes about music and dance and he also writes about television programs, the theater, films, and changes in the relationship of government to the arts.

His working day is "crazy and unpredictable," says Kriegsman. On one particular day he may start at nine thirty in the morning with a screening of a television program that will be on the air in the next week or so and he is very likely to have an evening assignment the same day so that he doesn't finish until one in the morning. In between he may be working on a long-term assignment, reading through music and film magazines or covering a breaking story which suddenly materializes and which an editor assigns to him.

One of his long-term assignments was a study of cable television: its successes, its problems, and its future prospects. For a while he was covering the District of Columbia Commission on the Arts and Humanities which was being reorganized and had applied for a large sum of money from the federal government.

Because of the unpredictability of assignments Kriegsman never knows very far ahead of time what his schedule is going to be. "We spend a lot of our time working up schedules," he says, "but the way events break just doesn't allow for that kind of solid prediction, so last-minute changes are a way of life."

The kind of story that Kriegsman is most comfortable with is what journalists call a "think" piece. As he puts it: "I suppose I'm not naturally outfitted with the basic journalist's lust for news and for breaking stories, going out and digging out the facts and all that. I'm really someone who likes to contemplate and to make connections between perhaps remote things that people wouldn't think of putting together, or looking into the crystal ball and sort of trying to guess trends or to see trends that are developing that haven't been realized yet."

On one occasion he did a Sunday piece making those remote connections among six performances of films and plays which he happened to have seen within the previous two weeks. These works probably did not have any intrinsic connection, Kriegsman observed, except for the fact that he had seen them all within a two week period. Nevertheless, he created a thoughtful and absorbing article about the relationship between costliness of production and quality, the most luxurious productions being the most superficial and the least glamorous being the ones most nearly approaching true art.

Kriegsman's interest in writing contemplative articles undoubtedly stems from his academic background, although he never felt really comfortable in the academic world, doing meticulous, scholarly historical research. He did enjoy teaching, however, and he sees his work as a critic in some ways related to teaching. As a teacher he was performing live on a small stage, whereas when he writes criticism he has very little sense of how his work is received. The lack of feedback he finds frustrating but, on the other hand, he likes responding to a new situation each time he has an article to write, unlike a classroom syllabus where the material is basically the same from semester to semester. He finds that even when he is seeing the same Shakespeare play or hearing the same Mozart symphony for the umpteenth time, the performance and the experience of writing about it are fresh and new each time.

Another difference between the newspaper and

academia is deadline pressure. Kriegsman, being a contemplative man, does not enjoy having to turn out a review in one hour after an evening performance. When he worked for the *San Diego Union*, even though it was a morning paper, he rarely had to write a review for the next morning's edition because San Diego is such a spread-out community that it was almost always impossible to get back to the office in time.

The *Post* was a rude shock. Kriegsman recalls the first time he had to do an evening review he had forty-five minutes of writing time and "was sweating bullets." He had four reference books, copious notes from the concert and an elaborate outline. About ten minutes after he had started work, Paul Hume, the lead music critic, came in from his assignment. Hume had no books and no notes; he paused to talk to someone at another desk; he picked up a magazine and leafed through it. Then he sat down and turned out a polished, articulate, beautifully organized article in less than half an hour.

Kriegsman has learned to cope with deadlines but he still is not happy with them. He acknowledges, however, that he often turns out a better piece of writing under tight deadline pressure than when he has days to do a story.

The changeover from the old entertainment section to Style brought more pressure. "Madness," Kriegsman called it, "total madness. Everybody felt that it was a great idea but nobody knew really how to get it going." He explained that under the old system people wrote reviews the way they had always been written and no one questioned this way of doing things. Under the new regime everything was being examined and questioned and looked at afresh. Editors were charged up with new ideas and writers were shaken out of their old patterns.

Eventually, Kriegsman says, "We settled down to a sort of routine madness."

During nonworking hours Kriegsman finds that he is always analyzing performances and sometimes he is even unconsciously taking notes. But the habit of analyzing does not detract from his enjoyment of a good performance. "I find I can be emotionally gripped and immersed and held and at the same time my mind is seeing things and making connections," he says.

Kriegsman and his wife share their professional and avocational interests in films and television. Mrs. Kriegsman was an editor at the American Film Institute and a writer herself. Her husband says, "She is my critic and she is very severe. I don't really feel that I've done anything worthwhile unless she says so. Too often I've been pleased with something initially and she'll be critical of it. Then weeks later when I come back and look at it I realize she was right."

Kriegsman considers that his specialty as a critic is having no specialty; he writes about films, television, dance, theater, sometimes separately and sometimes in combination. This kind of versatility and breaking down of stereotyped ways of writing about the arts are some of the things that Style is trying to encourage.

One area which has remained more traditional than the rest of Style is the book section. The *Post* puts out a Sunday section called Book World and there is always a book review in the daily paper.

The editor of the book section is William McPherson, who began his writing and editing career as a copyboy in the *Post*'s women's section after graduating from the University of Michigan. He and Judith Martin were contemporaries and she recalls that they were the two worst spellers on the paper. McPherson was the only male reporter in the women's section for a while and then he was put in charge of the travel department. Subsequently he went to New York as an editor with William Morrow, the publishing company, and after several years there, he was invited back to the *Post* to become editor of a Sunday book magazine called Book World, which had been a joint production of the *Post* and the *Chicago Tribune* and which the *Post* took over completely in 1970.

Book World was a sixteen-page tabloid, a sizable publication to put out every week. By 1973 Book World was running into trouble with the advertising department which felt that it was not producing enough revenue to justify the cost of putting it out. A newspaper of the stature of the *Post* could not be without a book section, however, so Book World was transformed to make it more economical. It was stretched from tabloid to full-page size and cut from sixteen tabloid pages to eight newspaper size pages. It was also inserted as a pull-out into the middle of the Sunday Style section where it was felt that it would be seen by more readers and would therefore be a better advertising medium.

So now Book World is something of an autonomous unit within Style. The book reviews appear in Style but McPherson runs his own department and does not report to the Style editors, except to turn in daily book reviews.

McPherson, a slim, dark haired man in his late thirties, supervises a staff of seven people in the tasks of filing books that come in to be reviewed, assigning them to reviewers, sending them out to be reviewed, editing reviews, doing art work, dealing with production and layout.

Book World receives about three hundred books a week from publishers who want them to be reviewed. McPherson's small office is packed with books. The shelves, covering one wall, are filled and more books are piled waist-deep on the floor in front of the shelves. The book titles are filed according to date of publication and McPherson reads trade publications and catalogues to decide which books should be reviewed. Then he tries to find guest reviewers who would be suitable to review the books.

Most of Book World's reviews are done by people outside the *Post*: professors, writers, specialists who seem particularly qualified to review a certain book. Sometimes staff members write reviews themselves. McPherson would like to do more writing than he does but he finds it difficult to free himself from administrative chores.

McPherson has strong ideas about the purpose of a newspaper book review section and what it should try to achieve. First of all he thinks that book reviews should educate and inform the general reader, that they should not be written for specialists. He tries to achieve a balance in each issue so that books on a variety of subjects are reviewed each time. He also sees the reviews which he publishes as part of a larger picture. A book will be reviewed in a number of publications and each review will have something different to contribute to an understanding of the book.

Then there is the question of which books to review. "We don't do unfavorable reviews of bad books," McPherson says. "There's no point in clubbing a guy to death." Sometimes problems arise for McPherson when he receives a book to review which has been written by a friend. Since he worked for a publishing company as an editor, he of course knows many writers and feels a certain amount of pressure when their books are to be reviewed. "Some papers have a whole system of cronyism," he says, "but that sure as hell is not the way we operate."

On one occasion the first book of a friend of his received an unfavorable review, which McPherson published. When her second book came out, he gave it to a reviewer, told her the book was written by a friend and asked her to tell him what she thought of it before she wrote her review, which turned out to be favorable.

He tries not to assign reviews to friends of the author of the book being reviewed if he can help it.

When *Post* staff members or prominent political figures write books, there is a certain amount of pressure to publish a favorable review. But McPherson often doesn't review the book at all if he doesn't think it is important; if a reviewer turns in an unfavorable review, it is published. "You get sort of hardened to being criticized for this," McPherson said, and then he paused. "Well, never completely hardened," he added.

Another problem which he is aware of as a book editor is the transience of what appears in a newspaper. "You're caught up in the evanescent," he says, "and there's a danger of hyping everything up. But on the other hand if you say, 'Here is a book which is neither the best nor the worst of its kind,' then the reader can say, 'Why are you wasting my time?'"

The problem is how to think of something to say without saying that a particular book is the greatest of its kind. It means having to be aware of trends without being caught up in them and carried away by a book which will be of no interest in a year.

For someone who likes books and enjoys reading, it can be frustrating to be a book editor. "I never finish a book," McPherson says. Several years ago he had an operation on his knee and had to stay in bed for several weeks recuperating. One of the pleasures of his convalescence was reading, reading books from cover to cover that had nothing to do with his job, books that were ten years old, twenty years old, that he didn't have to make decisions about.

Whether a critic is dealing with new ways of writing criticism as Kriegsman is or with a more traditional format as McPherson is, critics have some characteristics in common. They need to have the qualities of fairness, judgment and balance and they must look at trends in the arts without being caught up and carried away by them. Finally, both these critics are able to regenerate enthusiasm for their subject matter and for writing about it and this is perhaps the most important quality of all.

CHAPTER 13

Magazine Within a Newspaper

*I*n the fall of 1966 an article appeared in the *Post*'s Sunday magazine section, Potomac, about campus life at the University of Virginia. The author was a student at the University with a name that had the ring of the old Southern aristocracy, Shelby Coffey. The picture next to his biographical sketch showed a dark-haired young man with sullen eyes and a slightly pouting mouth.

It was something of a fluke that Shelby Coffey, III, was asked to write the article on "the last of the old broken-down Bourbon prep schools," the reputation of the University of Virginia at the time. Walter Pincus, a bright and ambitious young journalist whom Bradlee had hired to raise Potomac from its condition as a vapid showpiece for expensive full-color advertising, was looking around for lively subject matter and promising new writers. Shelby Coffey happened to be a friend of a friend of a friend whom Pincus had asked to find somebody at the University of Virginia who might be interested in writing an article. Since Coffey had written some fiction which had been published in the college literary magazine, he seemed to be a likely prospect. Pincus accepted the article and Shelby Coffey began to have visions of a career as a writer.

He wrote another Potomac piece on the landed aristocracy of Albemarle County, Virginia, and then at the end of his junior year in college, he applied for a summer job at the *Post*. Walter Pincus tried to get him hired as a summer intern on the Potomac staff but Potomac was not given an intern that year. The next best thing Pincus could do for his young protégé was to assign him some freelance articles.

Coffey wrote four or five articles that summer at $100 for a four or five thousand word piece. He survived by staying in various friends' apartments rent-free while they were on vacation and by getting occasional subsidies from his father, a lawyer in Chattanooga, Tennessee.

One of the articles he wrote was about surfers at Rehoboth Beach, Delaware. He was trying hard to achieve the flair of a Tom Wolfe or a Gay Talese but he was hung up with the rather ponderous classical symbolism of his college English courses.

". . . the girls of summer come to honey their flesh," he wrote, "to straw their hair, and to burn away the memory of the pale and chastely winter. Bacchus reigns and Aphrodite wears a two piece."

And he concluded his piece with an overwritten line that echoed Herman Melville and Alan Ginsberg: "And there it is—the lone mystically intense figure turning amidst the whirling seas on an alabaster, man-made board beneath the burning tangerine eye of God."

Shelby Coffey was straining to become a magazine writer at a time when magazine journalism was breaking traditions, exploring new subject matter and new methods. Dropping the pretense that a writer could be objective or value-free, writers like Tom Wolfe, Jimmy Breslin, and Norman Mailer gloried in the personal pronoun and made their own reactions and their involvement with the subject matter the heart of their reporting.

The "New Journalism" caught on and one of its creations was *New York*, a forum for the best of the

New Journalists. And Potomac under Walter Pincus was a part of the New Journalism. Pincus and Clay Felker, the editor of *New York*, were friends and shared many of the same ambitions for their publications. Potomac, of course, was hampered by budgetary limitations; Pincus could not offer his writers what Felker was paying but he managed to assemble a stable of lively Washington writers who made the magazine one of the first sections that readers would pick up on Sunday morning.

By June 1968 when Shelby Coffey graduated from college and came back to Washington to try for a permanent position with the *Post*, Walter Pincus was no longer editor of the magazine. He had gone on to become a staff writer in the news section of the paper and, later, executive editor of the *New Republic*.

Coffey, armed with his sheaf of Potomac articles, applied to Ben Bradlee for a job. Bradlee put him off but he kept persisting. Finally he was hired as a sports reporter and then about a month after he had joined the staff a writing job opened up at Potomac.

During the three years he spent there Shelby did a lot of writing on a variety of subjects. He learned to tone down his heavy symbolism and write more directly about what he saw. In January 1969 he wrote a piece about the town of Covington, Virginia, which was dominated by a mill which polluted the town with its smoke. First he evokes the look of the town: "Main Street . . . becomes a blurred image like a faded, aging photograph of the little town your grandfather talked about spending his hard but fair childhood in."

Then he describes the effect of the pollution: "Then comes the sense of claustrophobia. You can't get away from the smell, the haze, the feeling that your lungs are swallowing in some vaporous disaster. As if you stepped into a room where a hundred chainsmokers had just held a two-hour meeting."

After his three years as a writer and assistant editor at Potomac, Shelby went back to sports for a year, where he turned his writer's sensitivity to the lifestyles of athletic champions. What interested him about sports figures was what made them so good; what motivated champions and how did they respond to publicity, defeats, and victories.

While covering high school games and minor sports he occasionally had a chance to write a few pieces about the psychology of sports. "You'd see those stories every once in a while by some tire ad back on page D 21," he remarked wryly.

The fast pace, tight deadlines, and need for accuracy were good discipline, Coffey felt. He was glad to have the experience in the sports department but he didn't want to stay there forever. He didn't have to. He was soon tapped to become the editor of Potomac. He had been at the *Post* for four years and was barely 25 years old.

Now two years later he supervises a staff of eleven and puts out a magazine which usually runs between forty and sixty pages per issue. Coffey has an air of authority and control but he still looks like an Ivy League college boy of the 1960s: short dark hair with a forelock falling onto his forehead, crewneck sweater with rolled up sleeves, straight-legged, cuffed dark trousers, tasseled loafers very rundown at the heels. He speaks with a southern drawl and seems wary of being interviewed, a writer who is used to doing the interviewing himself and wants to control the situation.

Potomac's offices are on the fifth floor, down the hall from the newsroom. The large sunny room is partitioned at one end to make offices for Coffey and for the managing editor Marion Clark. The wall of Coffey's office is decorated with two portraits—an old king and an old tramp—and a photograph of a young man in a fancy-dress military uniform. Perhaps it is Coffey himself. In a bookcase there are stacks of *Sports Illustrated* and *New York* magazines and a few books, including *The Bureaucratization of the World, The Superlawyers*, and *Magazine Design.*

He is constantly dealing with a barrage of questions and administrative matters. The art director wants to know what has happened to a piece of art; a staff writer steps in and Coffey asks him to come back in the afternoon for a conference. "I don't understand what you wrote," he says. An artist with long hair in a pony tail brings in a collage of photos of politicians' wives. He places it on Coffey's desk and starts to leave.

"Are you coming back?" Coffey asks. "I want names on all these."

"You do?"

"Yes," Coffey replies firmly.

The phone rings. He makes a date for lunch at one o'clock.

Meanwhile, a woman on the staff is sitting at a desk in Coffey's office making telephone calls to obtain information for a survey on what wives are worth for the various jobs that they perform—from food buyer to bookkeeper to lover. She is calling up offices which offer such services and finding out how much they charge per hour. The grand total was finally tallied at $793.60 per week.

Most of Coffey's time is spent assigning articles, conferring with staff writers and freelancers, editing copy, and supervising production. The Potomac office is not as harried as the news room but it is a busy place. The weekly production schedule allows a little more leeway than on the daily news side. The staff comes in at ten thirty in the morning and leaves at seven in the evening. The writers are usually assigned articles long in advance and have time to finish them without putting in a lot of overtime. But Coffey often comes in on weekends to take care of production matters: making sure that copy is set and reading proofs.

The magazine itself is 11 by 12½ inches in size. The cover is usually a full-page color photograph illustrating a story inside. There are from forty to sixty pages per issue depending on the amount of advertising. More than half, sometimes as many as three-fourths, of the pages contain advertising. (The ratio of advertising to copy is worked out according to a formula developed by the advertising department.)

Potomac's mandate is to write features about Washington and its environs which can be stretched to include parts of North Carolina and Pennsylvania, where Washingtonians vacation. Stories have included "Political Wives" by freelancer Abigail McCarthy, the estranged wife of the former Senator; "Bargains in Used Everything," an annotated directory of second-hand stores in the Washington area; and "The Fire," about a Pentecostal church in the heart of one of the District of Columbia's black neighborhoods. Regular features include a restaurant column and a page of word games: crossword, acrostic and cryptogram. In addition, there are occasional special issues on fashion, home design, weddings and gardening.

Some of the story ideas come from Coffey and some come from the staff. There are five regular staff writers who have their own ideas, and there are also freelancers who come in with ideas, which are quite often accepted. One writer proposed a piece on the problems married women with children have in finding part-time work and how they can set up cottage industries in their homes. The idea was accepted because it seemed that it would have wide readership.

The magazine seems overwhelmed by the advertisements: full-page color photos of shoes, tableware, and women's clothing featured at local department stores; swimming pool ads; courses on hypnosis featuring large bold black type; an advertisement for a book about the Chinese exercise system Tai Chi, which has no illustration and looks at first glance like a page of the magazine's text.

Readers of the magazine have complained about the advertising. In a reader survey there were complaints that there was too much of it, that the stories were buried among the ads and that some of the advertisements were in bad taste. Coffey thinks that the quality of the advertising has improved since the survey. He has conferred with the advertising staff and they have agreed that they want an attractive, well-designed magazine, but the advertisements are still garish looking and jarring in their typefaces and design.

Potomac's deadlines are five weeks ahead of publication for color copy and four weeks ahead for black and white. The type is set in the *Post*'s composing room, proofread by the Potomac staff, and corrected by the printers. Then it is pasted up according to layouts designed by the Potomac and advertising production staffs. These paste-ups are then sent to Standard Gravure in Louisville, Kentucky, where it is printed by rotogravure.

Coffey, who started out as a writer, now spends most of his time on administrative matters and editing. He rewrites articles from time to time but he does not have the time to concentrate on writing a long article. As he puts it, "My own methods of working are such that I really sort of like to be monomaniacal, almost, about whatever story I'm writing."

His position epitomizes the dilemma of the writer who becomes an editor. Clearly he likes to write and he enjoyed writing for Potomac largely because he worked under editors whom he liked and respected. But if he had worked under editors with whom he did not get along he would have enjoyed writing much less. Now that he is an editor who controls what goes into the magazine, he looks at the position of a writer with some doubts as to whether he wants to be in that seat again. "When you're a writer, you're controlled in effect by someone else, unless you work out a very good niche for yourself."

He is still enthusiastic about magazine journalism and does not think the spark ignited by the New Journalists has died out. On the contrary, it has spread into daily newspapers as well. In the *Post*'s Style section, for example, detailed profiles are done of public figures, which try to get close to the person and show the human being behind the public façade.

Coffey may sometimes feel bogged down in details of administration and production but he doesn't forget that this is simply part of the responsibility of being an editor.

CHAPTER 14

"The Dropouts"

Besides having the same name and having his work appear daily in the *Post*, Howard Post has little to do with the newspaper. He is not on the staff, and he has never been introduced to the editors. When he does visit Washington, it is to tour the National Gallery with his wife and two daughters or to enjoy the cherry blossoms. Howard Post is the cartoonist who draws the comic strip called "The Dropouts."

Post lives in New Jersey near New York City and does all his work in New York. He has sold his strip to United Features Syndicate, Inc., which in turn sells and distributes it, as well as many other features, to newspapers all over the world.

Small newspapers which could not afford to hire an internationally known political columnist to write exclusively for them can buy a famous writer's column from the syndicate. The syndicate pays the columnists according to the number of newspapers it is able to sell.

In addition to comic strips and political columns, many other features are syndicated as well: advice columns such as Ann Landers, women's page features on sewing and housekeeping, articles about the stock market, humorous columns, crossword puzzles, children's stories, and puzzles. The intense public interest in our physical well being has inspired many syndicated columns by doctors on health care, nutrition, and even organic gardening.

It is felt by some media critics that syndication has

standardized newspapers around the country. A newspaper in Kansas has some of the same comics as the *Washington Post*. A bridge buff in Florida might be sweating over the same hand as his cold counterpart in Alaska. They feel that this trend is destroying the individuality of the local newspapers. Locally written stories are being displaced by syndicated articles and so might eliminate the vast training ground for newspaper people.

While syndicates are looking for work that is very good as well as for material that many newspapers all over the country will want to buy, it must meet a middle ground standard. On the other hand, if the syndicated material is better than what local writers could do, then it can be argued that syndication is improving newspapers.

It is not easy to break into writing or drawing cartoons for a syndicate. The competition is tough. Although thousands of cartoonists send their work to syndicates, only two or three new strips are accepted every year. Howard Post was one of the lucky ones with "The Dropouts," but his success came only after many years of hard work.

Post had always wanted to be a serious artist, but circumstances led him to cartooning. Alert junior high school teachers and his parents recognized his talent and urged him to apply to the High School of Music and Art in New York City, where he lived at the time. He was accepted and there he did what he liked best—drawing and painting. After graduation, Post continued his art education at Cooper Union School of Art.

It was a great disappointment that he had to leave Cooper Union before earning his diploma. "My father had to have an operation," he said. "It took him months to recover and of course he couldn't work, so I had to get a job to help support the family and pay the hospital bills."

The only job he could find that used his artistic talents at all was work as an in-betweener in a studio where animated cartoons were made for movies. An in-betweener is the low man on the totem pole in a cartooning studio. The main artist or animator does the drawings that initiate and end the action in each cartoon sequence. Then another artist does the intermediate action, and the in-betweener fills in all the steps between. For this Post earned $21 a week.

His first big break came when one of the men working with him as an in-betweener told him about a man who wanted someone to draw comic books for him. The man offered him $360 in advance to do the work. Post smiles as he remembers how excited he had been.

"I had never seen that much money before," he says. "I couldn't believe the check was real. I rushed over to the guy's bank to cash it right away."

He once worked for two years developing a strip with a serious story line about a prehistoric family. He spent days in the library looking up information about the shapes of people's heads, the kind of food they ate, what tools and weapons they used, and other details to make his drawings and narrative authentic. The editor at the syndicate told him that the strip was good but that it wasn't the right time to sell a strip based on that kind of subject.

Post was bitterly disappointed but the more he thought about the strip, the more he realized that he should have been doing something else. "I'm a humor man," he says now. "I've been doing humorous drawings all my life. So I scrapped the serious strip without taking it anywhere else and started on another one." But the seed idea for the new strip on primitive life had already taken root.

Since he had a family to support, Post couldn't drop everything and spend all his time working on the new strip. He was then earning his living by drawing the illustrations for comic books and occasionally doing some cartoons for television. He didn't particularly enjoy that work but until he could sell a strip of his own, there weren't many other opportunities for a cartoonist.

Post could spend only a few hours a day working on his new strip. He knew that a syndicate editor would want to see at least six weeks of the strips for both daily and Sunday papers, as well as an outline of some of the ideas he had for the future. It took him over two months to have enough finished drawings to take to New York, but on his first try he sold "The Dropouts" to the United Features Syndicate.

The new strip was centered around two men shipwrecked on a desert island. "They dropped out of society," Post says, "and had to make it on their own." He developed the strip by jotting down his humorous ideas, "shooting out humor tentacles," he calls it.

First, humor could center around the characters themselves—one tall, one short; one smart, one not so bright. Survival, getting food and shelter, were certainly basic problems for his two characters. He thought of many humorous situations that might develop around gardening, home building, fishing. Then there was the question of what they retained from their past life "in civilization" and what they wanted to include in building a new one: art, for instance, abstract painting on a desert island.

First he wrote an idea on a piece of paper and began to make a rough sketch:

Then he did a more finished pencil drawing, wrote in the balloons with the characters' speeches, and drew a border around the edge of each picture. The strip was then sent to a letterer who inked in the balloons and the borders and returned it to him:

Finally, he went over all his pencil lines with ink and pasted in strips of grey plastic tape made up of small black dots (benday) to shade in the areas the artist feels necessary. Then he erased all the pencil lines. The syndicate pasted its copyright mark in small letters at the bottom of the strip. This was the finished product:

As he was working out his humor situations he was developing his two characters. He named them Sandy and Alf. Alf is tall and skinny and always has bright ideas. Sandy is short and fat and he often shocks Alf with his simplemindedness. In one strip Sandy decides to plant banana seeds. Alf asks him if he is going to weed his banana patch. Sandy says yes. Then Alf asks him how he is going to know which little plants are bananas and which are weeds. "Oh, that's easy," Sandy replies. "When I see the bananas, I'll pull up all the others."

Post feels that there was only one drawback to signing a contract with the syndicate. "When I signed that contract," he says, "my characters didn't belong to me anymore. I had to sign them over to the syndicate and it has all rights to them. That's the way the business works. If I wanted to go to another syndicate, I would have to leave my strip with United Features because they hold the copyright."

He thinks that the system is basically unfair to cartoonists. Writers and musicians hold copyrights on what they write; why shouldn't the artist who draws a comic strip have the copyright, instead of the syndicate? But if he disagrees strongly enough with the system to refuse to be syndicated, there are thousands of other cartoonists who will gladly take his place and accept the syndicate's requirements.

Though selling the strip to United Features was indeed an accomplishment, Alf and Sandy were a long way from appearing in a newspaper. They had to be sold again and again and again, to as many papers as United could convince that the strip would tickle their readers.

At the *Post*, Jack Lemmon, night managing editor, was convinced. Lemmon's major responsibility is seeing that the news gets into print. The job of selecting the comic strips was dropped in his lap because he was there. If Howard Post were to draw his caricature, Lemmon might look very much like Sandy: short and stocky.

Lemmon is constantly receiving comic strips both from syndicates and individuals. Though the final decision is made by Simons, Bradlee, and Lemmon, the strip is passed around the office to get some feedback. The art director is usually asked for his artistic judgment as to form and style.

When asked in what direction he saw comic strips going, Lemmon pointed to "Doonesbury" as being controversial and topical. Though a number of letters have expressed displeasure with politics on the comic page, the strip has a large and appreciative following. There seems to be a trend away from adventure and continuity strips and toward an emphasis on the gaff.

On the other hand, the *Post* dropped Al Capp's "Lil Abner." Lemmon and the other editors thought it was offensive. "There were too many tasteless strips coming in from Capp. There was a character, Wonder Moron. We got a lot of letters objecting to his poking fun at the handicapped and retarded—he's also been offensive to the Indian as well." Lemmon and his colleagues liked Alf and Sandy and the two characters have been cavorting through the comic section of the *Post* for about six years.

Every week Post has to bring the syndicate six strips in black and white for the daily papers and one Sunday strip in color. For the black and white strips Post's deadlines are about five weeks before the strip is to appear in the newspaper. For the Sunday strips they are about two months ahead of the date when the strip appears.

The syndicate has everything worked out down to the smallest detail. Post is given special strips of paper to draw on. They are cut to just the right size so that the drawings can be reduced by a photographic process to the right length and width for a newspaper column.

Metal plates are made of the reduced drawings, each black line on the original drawing becoming a raised line on the metal plate. The engraver sends these plates back to the syndicate and they then go to the syndicate's own processing plant.

The processors take the heavy metal plates and roll cardboard sheets called mats over them under strong pressure. Then the strips are reproduced in as many copies as the syndicate needs on the lightweight cardboard mats and the mats are sent off to the newspapers in neat packages.

The newspaper editor in charge of the comic strip page can take the mat, which has a week's strips on it, cut off each day's strip and fit it into the makeup of the paper's comic page. The mats are specially treated to resist heat. To make a printed page from the mat, hot lead is poured into it and when the lead cools and hardens, a print is made from the lead cut. For Sunday color mats are made up.

Post was delighted the first time he saw "The Dropouts" in print. It was satisfying to see Alf and Sandy in black ink on the newspaper page, where they belonged, and to know that thousands of people would be able to enjoy their humor.

It wasn't long before he had concrete evidence that people were reading his strip. Letters began coming into the syndicate and Post picked them up on his weekly trips to deliver his work. Most of them were straightforward fan letters from people who enjoyed "The Dropouts" and wanted to tell him so. Other readers had special comments or criticism, though.

Many letters concerned the Dropouts' bathing suits. Some readers thought Sandy and Alf should wear briefer bathing suits or none at all. Others thought they should be more covered up. Readers seemed to notice even the smallest details. One man wrote that Post had drawn bananas growing in the wrong direction on a tree.

In another sequence Post had shown Sandy with a Venus flytrap plant which he was using to keep the flies off himself. One day a package arrived in the mail for Post and in it was a Venus flytrap sent by a reader.

One letter arrived from a woman who was teaching English to native Americans on a Navaho reservation in Arizona. She explained that she used comic strips as a teaching device to help her students learn English and that she was using "The Dropouts" in her classes. Post was pleased that the strip was being put to such good use and began corresponding regularly with the teacher.

Post works with one United features editor, Jim Freeman. "Jim's a good editor," he says, "but you know artists and editors are always at war with each other. I get frustrated every time I show Jim anything because he always finds a mistake. Letters are squeezed too close together or I've left out a question mark or something like that. Or else he says he wants to rearrange the order of my strips because he thinks the one with the weakest gag should go in on Saturday when the fewest number of people read the paper. I don't know what he's talking about. I never do a weak gag."

Post chuckles. "He can get on me all he wants about my little mistakes but I'll never forget one time when I was in his office and the whole place was in an uproar. It seems that they had forgotten to send out the Sunday color mats for Tarzan which were supposed to go to a newspaper in Pennsylvania. The mats were sent out Special Delivery at the last minute and the paper went to press with Tarzan in the Sunday comic section. After the papers had been distributed, one of the dealers noticed something funny. The syndicate had sent out the wrong mats. Tarzan was in Spanish."

Two of his good friends are John Prentiss and Leonard Starr. Both have their own syndicated strips. John does "Rip Kirby" and Leonard draws "On Stage." For several years the three men shared a studio in New York.

"John was always teasing me," Post recalls. " 'You don't have to work very hard,' he would say. 'All you have to do is draw those sloppy-looking characters with big feet. That doesn't take much effort. Now look at our strips. Our characters have to look like real people— even down to their fingernails. You and your big feet,' he would say."

Post laughs. "I'd tell him he could make all the cracks he wanted but my bigfoot drawings took just as much work as his did." And so the phrase "bigfoot" (which means a broad, humorous style of drawing to all cartoonists) was born.

Post finds it amusing that some cartoonists begin to resemble the characters they draw. He never knew Harold Gray, who created "Little Orphan Annie," but Tex Blaisdell who draws the strip now has a mop of kinky hair just like Annie and Tex's son Bruce resembles her even more with his curly red hair and round, steel-rimmed glasses.

One of Post's friends once saw him as a model for Alf: "There you are, tall and dark-haired and skinny, just like Alf." Post's short, plump wife Bobbie, who was standing nearby, said, "Well, if he's Alf, then I'm Sandy."

When asked what he doesn't like about his work, Post thinks for a moment. Then he says, "Well, there is one thing: the dead periods. They're terrible. Sometimes I run dry of ideas and can't think of another gag. But so far I've always managed to come up with something."

He remembers one dry period when he had done the first part of a week's series of strips based on Sandy's love of bananas. Three strips were finished but he had completely run out of ideas for the rest of the week.

"I was sitting at my drawing board in front of a white sheet of paper," he recalls. "My mind was completely blank. Then I began mulling over what I had been doing for the past 24 hours. Bobbie and I had gone out for dinner at another couple's house the night before. It had been a good meal: beef stroganoff, lots of rice, delicious salad, and cheese cake for dessert. I would have loved a second helping but I was beginning to get a little heavy. Bobbie took a second helping and I teased her about it on the way home. While I was thinking about that, I suddenly had an inspiration for the strip. Dieting—Sandy eating bananas and getting too fat and going on a diet. I jotted down about five ideas—being popular with women only if you're thin, physical fitness, diet pills, willpower, overeating as a deep psychological problem."

He did one strip which showed Sandy lying with his head against a rock as if he were on an analyst's couch. Alf was sitting on the other side of the rock saying, "You overeat to avoid confronting a deep-seated problem." Frame two showed Alf saying confidently, "What is your problem?" In frame three Sandy was stroking his chin thoughtfully and answering, "I'm too fat," while this time Alf was the one to look puzzled.

"Sometimes I think I'm crazy to put myself under this kind of pressure, working seven days a week with those terrible deadlines to meet," Post says. Then a little smile crosses his face. "But it is fun when you come up with a new idea. You think you'll never be able to think of another one but you always do."

CHAPTER 15

House Counsel

*T*he atmosphere of the seventh floor executive offices is very different from that of the fifth floor newsroom. The newsroom is a bustling, informal place where a stranger can walk around freely and talk to anyone. The furnishings are practical and sturdy—white plastic topped desks, swivel chairs, and tough black carpeting on the floor. The seventh floor is different. You walk off the elevator and face a glass door beyond which is an expanse of thick white carpeting and a double row of secretaries' desks. When you enter the room, the woman at the first desk raises an eyebrow inquiringly and asks whom you want to see. "Is he expecting you?" she wants to know.

The person being visited is Gerald Siegel, vice president and counsel for *The Washington Post*. Siegel is a small, thin man with tightly curled white hair and a broad flat face. He is wearing an olive green suit, a yellow V-necked sweater, and a bow tie.

He is sitting behind a large desk and motions his visitors to sit in arm chairs next to a round white table. On the other side of the room is a sofa to accommodate additional visitors.

The paraphernalia of the office give some clues as to Siegel's responsibilities. On a long table behind his desk are an electric calculator and framed photos of his children. The shelves on the wall over the table are filled with law books and on his desk is a stack of books topped by one on recycling newsprint. Papers on the desk are held down by a Kiwanis Club paperweight.

He is immediately suspicious of being interviewed. He wants to know who has authorized a book about the *Post* and whether Mrs. Graham knows about it. Finally his lawyer's mind seems satisfied and he consents to talk about his job.

First, he emphasizes that most newspapers do not have legal counsels on the staff and that those which do ask them to perform a variety of tasks, many of which are not necessarily connected with legal matters. His own major responsibility is the procurement of newsprint, which, of course, is one of the major needs of the newspaper. He took on this job in 1969 when the former secretary-treasurer of the company, who had been in charge of newsprint procurement, retired. Siegel had had some connection with newsprint procurement for about five years before that, starting with the *Post*'s purchase of a forty-nine percent interest in the Bowaters Mersey Company, a Canadian newsprint mill.

Another one of his functions is community relations —membership in such organizations as the National Conference of Christians and Jews, the Urban Coalition, and the board of Children's Hospital. He points out that there is a clear and substantial dichotomy between the news staff and the business staff in the matter of participation in community organizations. The *Post* as a corporation is represented in the community and makes financial contributions to the United Givers Fund and other charities but only members of the business staff participate in such activities. Editors and reporters on the news and editorial staffs generally avoid membership in community organizations because their involvement might influence their news or editorial judgment, and because members of the organization might put pressure on them to cover the organization extensively or favorably in the news or editorial columns.

Siegel noted that when he was chairman of a National Conference of Christians and Jews award dinner, there was not a word about it in the news columns of the paper. "They didn't regard it as a newsworthy event and we didn't ask them to so regard it," he said.

He speaks of his involvement in the community as any public spirited business person would. "I do what I think is important in the community . . . as a member of the *Washington Post* family," but he emphasizes that his involvement is in no way related to his concept or anyone's concept of what a newspaper should do as a news organ.

The responsibilities which Siegel has described are those which any executive might perform for a corporation but some of the other things which he does are more related to a lawyer's training. He advises the advertising, promotion, and circulation departments on contract matters which arise within their departments and he reviews advertising copy to be sure that the material does not contain legal objections. He is also occasionally consulted on questions of libel and invasion of privacy by the editors, although major legal issues involving the news department and all litigation are handled by an outside law firm retained by the *Post*.

The dealers who distribute the *Post* are independent contractors who sign contracts with the newspaper to do their jobs. These contracts are reviewed periodically and sometimes there are problems which arise concerning these contracts. Advertisers also sign contracts with the advertising department which Siegel may help in drawing up or about which there may be a problem or dispute from time to time.

When it comes to advertising content, he is most

frequently consulted on political advertising, advertising which contains a great deal of written material promoting a particular point of view, what the *Post* calls "reader-type advertising." The federal government has certain legal requirements for political advertising and the *Post* has its own standards and ground rules. For example, the newspaper has generally taken the view that it will not accept a reader ad which contains libelous material even though the libel is not actionable as a matter of law.

The *Post* has very strict standards of acceptability for all its advertising and turns down thousands of lines of advertising every year for various reasons: matters of law and matters of taste. Siegel is occasionally involved in these decisions if they involve a trademark or a copyright, a federal trade question, or a lottery question. (Advertising which contains a lottery cannot be accepted.)

The newspaper's legal position on advertising is that anyone who wants to advertise has a right to publish unless his right imposes materially on other people's rights, for example, the readers' rights to be free from a particular advertisement which may be offensive. Siegel explains that the law states that "we are the final judge of what is acceptable in the newspaper and we try to apply that as fairly and liberally . . . as we can."

Libel and invasion of privacy are other major legal issues facing a newspaper, with which Siegel has had some experience. At one time he held lectures on libel and invasion of privacy for the reportorial staff. He and a lawyer from outside the company made presentations and answered questions. They covered definitions of libel and invasion of privacy, which are very difficult to define from a legal point of view, and they tried to give practical advice to reporters and editors about how to avoid difficulty, how to recognize when they were getting into a dangerous area and, how to seek help at the right time before it was too late. He no longer conducts these lectures but he does give advice on these questions if he is consulted about a specific problem.

When major legal problems arise which involve the news department, the editors go directly to an outside firm, usually Williams, Connally and Califano, whose senior partner, Edward Bennett Williams, a well-known and very successful Washington attorney, is also a close friend of Bradlee's.

On big legal matters, such as the publication of the Pentagon papers and the Watergate reporting, lawyers from Williams, Connally and Califano are consulted, but their advice is not always followed. An account of the publication of the Pentagon papers written by Chalmers Roberts, one of the reporters involved, shows the conflict between the journalistic and legal ideas of what should be done.

The *Post* had obtained a copy of these papers, which were a detailed record of U.S. involvement in Vietnam, four days after the *New York Times* had begun printing them, in June 1971. Roberts, Bradlee, and a group of other editors and reporters were writing stories based on the papers in the library of Bradlee's house.

During the evening a proposal, apparently initiated by the lawyers, according to Roberts, was made that the *Post* not publish the story but notify the Attorney General that the *Post* had the papers and would publish them later. All the reporters and editors present resisted this proposal and the issue was finally resolved by Mrs. Graham who said, "I say we print," against the lawyers' advice.

The *New York Times* was ordered to halt publication after three issues of stories and the *Post* ran two stories before District Court Judge Gerhard Gesell issued a temporary restraining order, halting publication. The government contended that publication of the papers would damage diplomatic efforts to end the war. Roberts contended that the *Post*'s lawyers didn't understand the newspaper business and would not take the word of reporters and editors on how secret documents are used. The *Post* submitted affidavits citing how government officials often leak secret documents and other classified information to reporters when it serves their purposes.

The Supreme Court lifted the restraining order on June 30 and both papers went on to publish the Pentagon papers. But the government had enforced prior restraint on publication for the first time and the Supreme Court's ruling did not bar future bans on publication.

Roberts' account, in his autobiography, *First Rough Draft*, shows the tension between lawyers and news people on such an issue: the lawyers' caution and desire for compromise versus the newspeople's pragmatism and concern for protection of the free press.

Siegel was not involved in the *Post*'s Pentagon paper fight but he certainly shows a lawyer's caution and care in defining his terms precisely and refusing to discuss anything in a casual, offhand way. When he was talking about libel and invasion of privacy he was unwilling to give any specific examples of cases off the top of his head. The lectures which were given to the staff were carefully prepared in writing and only if he had researched facts in detail would Siegel be prepared to discuss specific cases or even detailed definitions.

Siegel is an Iowan who came to the *Post* after a legal career which combined an interest in government and in business. From law school he went to the Securities and Exchange Commission where he worked for five and a half years. Then he spent six years as counsel to the Senate Democratic Policy Committee under Lyndon Johnson and then he taught at the Harvard Business School for three years.

Since he has been at the *Post*, he has seen the company grow from a small and "close knit corporate community" to a large, sprawling organization and he feels a little nostalgia for the old days and the closer relationships that people had when the paper was smaller.

Siegel is enthusiastic about the newspaper business in general. "It's a very exciting business to be in," he says. "It doesn't afford quite the diversity, at least in my experience, as some of the jobs I've had in government but it is a unique kind of activity, the news business. You tend to cover everything, literally everything. That makes it anything but dull and boring."

CHAPTER 16

The Business of Selling

"*A*nybody who gets into this business that I'm in and doesn't believe that service is 75 percent of selling might as well try something else."

The person speaking is Jim Leonard who has been selling advertising for *The Washington Post* since 1964. He is a pleasant looking man in his late thirties, stylishly dressed in a brown suit accented by a dark yellow shirt and brown patterned tie. His hair is sculptured and his voice is resonant.

Leonard handles four big retail accounts for the Post: Hecht, Sears, Zayre, and Kann. Hecht and Kann are two local department stores and Hecht is the biggest single account that the paper has, over $3\frac{1}{2}$ million lines each year. Sears is a nationwide chain and Zayre is a discount store with headquarters in Boston, Massachusetts, which sells a wide range of products.

These are all stores which have been advertising in the *Post* for years, and, as Leonard puts it, "They know that we need them and they need us and we both know it." With that understanding then, Leonard's job is primarily to make sure that the relationship continues to function smoothly. This means a lot of paperwork, checking, and coordination. Every Sunday the *Post* runs preprinted inserts for advertising. In the mailroom where the papers are tied into bundles and prepared for the circulation department there is an automatic stuffing machine which can stuff 13 inserts into the paper. The *Post* has four of its own supplements which go into four of the pockets and it makes nine available to its customers for advertising supplements. These are very popular with advertisers because they are now considerably cheaper than sending a similar leaflet through the mail, since bulk mailing rates have gone up.

Sometimes these inserts are reserved six months in advance and one of Leonard's responsibilities is to make sure that his clients know when dates are available and to make reservations for them. Then he has to check to make sure that the customers meet the *Post*'s deadlines and get their copy in on time. And he has to make sure that the *Post*'s production department, which does the layouts and sets the copy for ads, has the right dates and all the correct information necessary.

For example, on March 1 he found a slip of paper called an insertion order scheduling a Hecht Company ad for Sunday, March 31. This puzzled him because ads are not scheduled that far in advance. When he checked with the production department he found that someone had added on an extra digit and that the ad was supposed to be scheduled for Sunday, March 3 instead of Sunday, March 31. This meant that he had to work out some kind of arrangement with the production department to get the ad into the paper. Hecht's wanted it in the Style section which had already closed. It could be put into the front section but he would have to call the advertising director at Hecht's and see if that was all right. This was all part of a day's work for Jim Leonard.

More frequently than everyone would like, mistakes do occur. An advertisement appears in the wrong section or the address of a store is left out or a price is written $19.99 instead of $9.99. If one of these things happens to an ad placed by one of Leonard's clients, the phone on his desk is usually ringing by nine o'clock on the morning when the ad appeared. Then Leonard has to calm the angry advertiser and negotiate a settlement which will compensate him for the mistake.

He feels that this ability to placate an irate advertiser by a quick correction at minimal cost is an art that has to be learned.

The *Post*'s rate card says that the paper is responsible only for the space contained by the mistake but if the price is quoted incorrectly or left out completely, usually the paper will rerun the ad as quickly as possible. If the ad lists five addresses and one of them is incorrect, then the advertiser might be compensated for one-fifth of the space of the advertisement. Much of Leonard's time is spent in this kind of negotiating, rather than the kind of selling that one usually associates with advertising.

The large department stores which he deals with do not need much persuasion to advertise in the *Washington Post*, with one exception. When he took over the account for Kann's department store several years ago, 55 percent of the store's business was going to the *Evening Star*, possibly reflecting the conservative management's opinion of the *Post*'s editorial policy. The management changed and Leonard made a point of being available and helpful. Within months the *Post* was carrying 51 percent of Kann's business.

The *Post* does not sell advertising the way New York advertising agencies do, with elaborate presentations before a group of clients and wining and dining of customers at three-hour, three-martini lunches. Leonard says most of the store managers and advertising directors he deals with are too busy to go out to lunch, although he occasionally invites someone to the advertising club of Washington if there is an interesting guest speaker.

Likewise, he is rarely called upon to do a formal

presentation to a client but he likes to do one from time to time to keep from getting rusty. Zayre usually asks him to come up to Massachusetts once a year or so to keep its executives up to date. This means that he goes to Ron Browne, the *Post*'s research director and gets material pertinent to the account—this may be the figures on how many government people read the *Post* every day, circulation figures in various parts of the Washington metropolitan area, and, particularly for Zayre, figures on how many people with incomes between six and fifteen thousand dollars read the *Post* because this is the income group that Zayre is trying to reach. So he prepares folders of material to distribute, does an oral presentation, and answers questions.

Leonard works in the retail advertising section in a large open office on the sixth floor, which advertising shares with circulation and promotion. Retail has the largest volume of sales and the greatest amount of lineage in the advertising department. (Newspaper advertising is measured in agate lines, agate being the smallest size type face.) Next comes classified, then general, then automotive, then financial.

Automotive and financial are more or less self-explanatory categories. Automotive ads—tires, automobile parts, motorcycles and other vehicles as well as cars—usually appear in the sports section. Financial ads—brokerage firms, banks, savings and loan—as well as advertisements for office space and all other real estate are usually found in the financial section.

General or national advertising appears all over the paper. The rates for general advertising are substantially higher than those for retail. Retail rates are available only for advertisers who are dealing directly with consumers within the *Post*'s retail rate area which is the District of Columbia, Maryland, Virginia, Delaware, and West Virginia. Any advertiser within that area who is not dealing directly with the public pays the national rate.

Political ads and advertisements which the staff refer to as ax grinders fall into the general category. These are the most difficult advertisements to handle since they are usually expressing opinions forcefully on controversial subjects such as the Vietnam war, impeachment of President Nixon, the death penalty, or legalized abortion.

Each one of these ads must be approved by the advertising manager, the vice president in charge of advertising, and Gerald Siegel, the legal counsel. The paper takes very seriously its obligation to print all kinds of material, whether it agrees with the advertiser's viewpoint or not, and considers the advertisement carefully for content and taste. If an advertisement is making a personal attack on someone, the paper is not likely to print it.

Bob McCormick, the advertising manager, gave one example of the kind of problem the paper has to deal with in ax grinder ads. There is one particular person who frequently submits advertisements on the subject of law and order. In one he referred to muggers, rapists, and homosexuals, "All of whom," he said, "God intended should suffer the death penalty." McCormick was emphatic that this statement could not run as it was written and that the author of the advertisement would have to remove homosexuals from the category of muggers and rapists and would have to soften his language somewhat. The advertising department has two people who spend much of their time making such considerations and negotiating with the authors of ax grinders.

The classified department is the second biggest earner

of revenue after retail. In the classified sales room close to 100 people sit at desks with typewriters in front of them and telephone headsets over their ears taking down advertisements which come in over the phone. During an average week more than 15,000 calls come in over the automatic call distributor which counts the calls and holds them in order if all the telephone lines are occupied.

The manager of the classified advertising department is Scotte Manns, a woman who came to the *Post* with three years of experience in classified sales at the *Des Moines Register-Tribune* and has worked her way up to her present position during the ten years she has been at the *Post*. She supervises a staff of some 150 people—the salespeople on the telephones, salespeople who work on the street, copy editors, supervisors.

The classified department runs its own training program where new sales people are taught the mechanics of selling classified advertising, the *Post*'s policies on what is acceptable and what is not, and how to sell classified advertising space. The selling often comes in by way of persuading the advertiser to buy more linage than he had originally intended or to buy white space to set off his ad.

When most people think of classified advertisements, they think of an individual placing an ad to sell a car or a litter of puppies, or an employer placing an ad for an employment vacancy. But classified advertising also has its regular large customers who maintain accounts and sometimes buy as much as half or three-quarters of a page of advertising space—automobile dealers selling a number of used cars, a real estate firm with many houses on the market, a large company with a number of job openings—and a full page of classified advertising would cost about $4000.

Scotte Manns is one of the few women in an executive position on the business side of the paper and she has become an executive in a department which has traditionally been considered a women's field, although an increasing number of men are coming into it now. The telephone salespeople used to be called solicitors, a word which had rather unsavory connotations, implying that the person was dialing at random, using a hard-sell approach. Scotte Manns is pleased that the terminology has been changed and that more respect is being accorded to classified salespeople.

"We have many women who have made classified their career and I think anything that is done to elevate this or put it truly in the important perspective in which it belongs benefits everyone."

There are a number of problem areas which apply to all advertising—what kind of subjects to accept or reject, what kinds of standards to maintain. The *Post* advertising department puts out a thick booklet entitled, "The *Washington Post* Advertising Standards of Acceptability," which lists in detail what is acceptable and what is not. The booklet is revised frequently to keep up with changing mores.

For example, any advertisement which looks like an editorial or a news story must be marked "advertisement" and it must not use the type faces which are used in the editorial and news columns. No advertising for fortune tellers, hypnotists, or astrologers is accepted. Handguns may not be advertised and shotguns and rifles must be advertised as hunting or sportsmen's guns. No other advertising for weapons is acceptable.

Advertisements on the amusement pages of the paper must not contain material unsuitable for children, the rationale being that the *Post* is essentially a family-oriented newspaper and that the amusement advertisements are read by all age groups, whereas critiques and reviews on the news pages are generally not aimed at a young audience.

There are also no personal advertisements, such as "Susie, come home; all is forgiven" or "Male, age 30, looking for female companion." As Bob McCormick, the advertising manager, puts it, "If you were comparing us to most papers around the country, I think you'd have to call us purists."

Newspaper readers are often suspicious that large advertisers influence what goes into a paper's news columns. The *Post*'s management, on both the news side and the advertising side, insist that advertisers have no influence on news coverage. Bob McCormick says that he often hears complaints from advertisers about editorials or columnists or the paper's coverage of Watergate or other matters and some businesses have cancelled their advertising. But he says that he always tells them, "Up on the sixth floor here, our business is to sell advertising. If the *Washington Post* is an effective advertising medium for you and the economics say, 'Advertise in the *Washington Post*,' then you should advertise in the *Washington Post*. If you're buying our editorial policy, you're in the wrong ball park to start with."

McCormick says that much of this sort of complaining has subsided in recent years, perhaps because advertisers have simply recognized that they cannot change the paper's editorial stance, perhaps because they have recognized that the paper is an effective advertising medium with the largest circulation in the Washington area. But on the other hand, a different sort of criticism has started to surface—consumers complaining to the editorial department about the advertisements, the subject matter, the wording, the quality, the size. The managing editor always refers these complaints to the advertising department and nowadays McCormick finds that he has more of these complaints to deal with than he does from advertisers.

Two examples can give a sense of how advertising and news are intertwined. During the gasoline shortage of the winter of 1974 the oil companies began taking out advertisements insisting that they were not taking excessive profits and cheating the public and criticizing the government for controlling the price of oil and natural gas. Mobil ran one of these ads in Outlook, the *Post*'s Sunday news supplement, on March 10, 1974.

Two days later a news story appeared on the first page of the Style section quoting a statement by Representative Benjamin Rosenthal of New York, requesting free television and radio time to rebut such advertisements and encouraging newspapers and magazines to give free space to interested parties for the same purpose.

The article quoted various individuals representing pros and cons on the issue and the Mobil ad was mentioned. However, it was not mentioned that the ad had run two days earlier in the *Post*. In the middle of the article the *Post*'s vice president for advertising, Joseph Lynch, is quoted as saying that the newspaper's policy is not to provide free space for counter advertising. If the corporation pays for its advertisement, then the respondent should also pay, he said.

The article leads off with material criticizing the oil companies and then, in traditional newspaper fashion, presents other points of view on the subject. The initial impression that the article gives, though, is that the oil companies are being criticized. All the critical material appeared on the front page while the rebuttals were jumped to the inside.

In this particular case the article and the advertisement probably had no connection. The editor who assigned the story and the reporter who wrote it may not have even noticed the Mobil ad in the Sunday paper. They were prompted to write the story by Representative Rosenthal's statement.

The other example involves a long-term relationship between the real estate section of the paper and the advertisers in that section. Every Saturday the *Post* publishes a thick real estate section which is put out by an editor and a part-time reporter. Because the staff is so small, the editor depends heavily on handouts and press releases sent in by large developers, home builders' associations, real estate boards, and the like. Articles are also written by outside contributors who are willing to work for the *Post*'s low freelance rates. These tend to be people like mortgage bankers, the president of the National Association of Home Builders, a Virginia Real Estate Commissioner, and other pillars of the home building industry establishment. This is one place in the paper where advertisers get their point of view into the news columns because the paper has not allocated enough money to the real estate section for it to do very much independent reporting.

For a person who is interested in newspaper sales, the *Post* is a good place to work. For one thing the salaries are good. All the sales people are represented by the Newspaper Guild, the same union which represents the news staff, and the salary scales are the same as those for reporters. A fully experienced salesperson earns as much as a fully experienced reporter, which is over $400 a week, and a fully experienced classified telephone sales person earns nearly $300 a week. At many newspapers the salespeople receive bonuses or commissions for selling but the *Post* does not operate under this system.

Jim Leonard likes selling at the *Post*. He finds that he works well when he is on a salary but he is not the kind of person who could go door to door and use the high pressure tactics that people use when they are selling encyclopedias or storm windows on straight commission.

He hastens to add that being on a straight salary does not mean that salespeople can sit back and relax. "You're not watched like a hawk," he says, "because they have figures at the end of the month they can look at. If these figures are bad, then you're not doing your job or you've got to get in and defend the fact that Korvette has just pulled 100,000 lines out of the *Washington Post*."

Korvette did pull a lot of advertising out of the *Post* soon after Leonard took over the account. The reason was that they were making cutbacks in the entire chain of stores, not that Jim Leonard was dropping the ball, but he had to hurry to his supervisor's office to explain this.

During his working day Leonard can set his own pace. No one is standing over his desk telling him what to do or watching the clock and he appreciates the independence that he has.

"If you want to take a client out for a two hour lunch, if you need it you've got it. If you get stuck in a traffic jam and don't get in till ten o'clock, just make sure you return all those calls that are waiting for you on your desk."

Leonard's day starts at six-thirty in the morning in his suburban Maryland home when he gets up before his wife and two children to have a quiet cup of coffee and read the paper by himself. He likes to know what is in the paper before he goes to work so that he isn't hit cold when he gets to the office with a major mistake that he hasn't even seen.

By eight o'clock he is ready to leave home for the 21 mile drive into Washington. He has outfitted his Chrysler Newport with an AM/FM stereo radio and a rack on the door for a coffee cup to make his ride to work more pleasant. He slides his car into the *Post* parking lot and gets to his desk a little before nine to try to organize his day before the phone starts ringing.

Leonard came into his job at the *Post* quite by accident. His first love was radio and he was a disc jockey in Wildwood, New Jersey, from 1960 to 1962. However, the market was saturated with aspiring disc jockeys at that time and Leonard couldn't make it on $85 a week.

His fiancée, now his wife, lived in Washington, so he came down to look for a job. He saw an advertisement in the *Washington Post* for sales personnel, applied for the job, and was hired. Ten years later he is satisfied to be where he is, assistant manager of chain and department store advertising. As for the future, he could see himself moving up in the *Post* hierarchy or becoming the manager of an advertising staff of a chain of suburban newspapers.

He likes his job; he likes Washington. When he looks back, he has no regrets. "I've found a home here," says Jim Leonard.

CHAPTER 17

The Miracle on Fifteenth Street

*E*very day about 1500 people in the production department work in shifts around the clock to assemble all the pieces and produce the daily newspaper.

The operation is so complex, with so many opportunities for snags, foul-ups, and even major catastrophes, that people all over the building are amazed that the paper gets put out every day. "The miracle on Fifteenth Street," it is sometimes called.

Advertising copy has to be ready long before the deadline. Salespeople in the advertising department tell their clients that all copy has to be in by Monday night in order to meet the deadline for Friday morning's paper. When the advertising copy comes in, it is sent to the publications department, logged in on the advertising manifest book, and sent on to the proper place depending on how much work the advertiser has already done on it.

Then a compositor assembles the various parts of the ad, the artwork and the written copy, and pastes the pieces into the format indicated by the advertiser's original drawing. The paste-up is sent to the composing room where it is electrostated. A sample of the ad, called a proofsheet, is printed up for the advertiser to look at and correct if necessary.

All this work takes place on Tuesday. The people on the late night shift, from one thirty a.m. till nine a.m., called the lobster shift, do the final work so that the proofsheets are ready to be delivered to the advertisers at nine o'clock on Wednesday morning. The advertisers have all day Wednesday to correct the proofs and send them back by six o'clock Wednesday evening. Meanwhile the printers and compositors are working on advertisements for Saturday and Sunday. Sunday, of course, is a particularly heavy day, so preparation of Sunday ads goes on all through the week.

On Wednesday, the night shift of makeup people, who work from four in the afternoon until midnight, dummy the ads. On sheets of paper the size of a newspaper page, with lines indicating the width of newspaper columns, ads for Friday's paper are laid out, leaving space at the top of the pages for the news stories.

By Thursday noon the dummies are sent upstairs from the makeup department on the fourth floor to the fifth-floor newsroom. There night managing editor Jack Lemmon and his staff are going through the news budgets from the various departments—national, Metro, Style, sports, financial—to choose stories for the various pages. Lemmon has already made up a news budget for the whole week, and the various departments have to fit into their allocation. The rest of the paper consists of advertisements, as many pages as necessary but not according to a specific percentage formula.

We have already seen in Chapter 2 how the front page is laid out. The rest of the pages are done in similar fashion by members of the news desk staff. The second and third pages are reserved for important world news. As the dummies are made up, headline sizes are chosen and headline writing is assigned to editors on the copy desk who are reading the copy that filters in by the seven forty-five deadline.

As deadline time approaches, the pace quickens. Released ad paste-ups of advertising copy set during the day are being photographed and engraved on metal plates. Downstairs, where the electronic typesetting machines and makeup room are, activity is now hurried in the paste-up and closing out of all the classified pages that have been set on the electronic phototype setting machines during the day shift. Now activity is picking up in the linotype section, where news copy is set. The printers, or linotype operators, are working rapidly on the news copy that is coming down from the fifth floor.

The linotype process of typesetting is also called hot type because the operator works a keyboard which imprints the characters on a hot lead block called a slug. The slugs drop out of the machine with the whole typed story imprinted (in reverse) in the type size and column width that will appear in the paper.

The printers are clattering away at their keyboards at the bank of machines on one side of the room. Meanwhile, chases (metal trays which hold the linotype slugs and photoengraved plates of advertising and photographs) have been set up on long tables, and members of the page makeup staff are fitting in the advertising plates according to the instructions on the dummy sheets.

As the printers finish their stories, they are printed up on long sheets of paper and sent across the room on an overhead conveyor belt to the proofreaders, who correct the proofs and return them, with the slugs, to the printers to be redone.

By seven forty-five all the copy except for a few late items is supposed to be down in the composing room. Lemmon keeps checking to make sure that the flow of work is smooth, so the printers will not be overwhelmed at one point and idle at another.

At seven o'clock Jack Lemmon goes out for dinner but the printers have reached the busiest part of their day. Machines are clattering and people are running back and forth between the linotype machines and the chases. Printers and makeup editors are bent over the chases, studying dummies and fitting type into holes.

"Hey, Joe," one of the printers calls across the room. "I've got a story that won't fit."

Joe, the makeup editor, comes over to deal with the problem. He studies the slug which is about an inch too long. Over the years he has become experienced in reading backwards. "Bite the last graph," he says to the printer. The printer slices off the last paragraph and the story fits.

A few pages are finished. As they are completed the printers tighten bolts around the edges of the chases to lock in the type. Then they raise a little metal flag on the side of the chase. This is a signal that it is locked up and ready to go to the stereotyping department. The chases are slid from the tables onto wheeled tables and taken off to be stereotyped.

In the stereotyping process the chase full of metal slugs and photoengraved plates is impressed under high pressure into a thick wood fiber mat which is then molded into a curved shape to fit the shape of the press cylinder. Then a heavy metal plate is made from the fibrons mat. This is the plate that fits onto the press. Three to four presses are needed to do a normal run for the Capital Edition, the first of the three editions of the paper done each night. Thus, from 400 to 800 plates, depending on the number of pages, are cast between the time the paper goes to bed and the time the press run begins—a period of less than three hours between seven-thirty and ten-fifteen in the evening.

Now the action shifts to the ground floor pressroom where pressmen are fitting the plates onto the presses, putting the huge rolls of paper into position, adjusting knobs, pulling levers, seeing that rollers are in the proper position. Finally everything is ready. The night foreman pulls the master switch and the presses are rolling. The paper starts moving through the huge rollers along the bank of press units which extend from one end of the building to the other, about half a city block.

The newspapers start coming out at the end of the press, cut and folded by machine. Then a conveyor belt carries them up to the next floor where the mailers are supervising automatic stacking and tying machines which pack the newspapers into uniform size bundles to be ready for the dealers to pick up for distribution. Here the responsibility of the production department ends and the circulation department takes over.

After the Capital Edition the printers go out for supper and a few beers. Then they come back to put together the second edition, called the Two Star Edition. This usually involves only minor changes: one or two stories on the front page may jump to an inside page, a few late sports scores may be added.

The Three Star Edition closes at midnight and this usually involves setting a lot of type and changing more pages—front page news stories, night sports events, theater and concert reviews in the Style section. The Final Edition is replated by the people on the lobster shift. This is not usually a major project for them unless there is a big story breaking after midnight.

A thumbnail sketch of the production process does not do justice to what actually happens—the snags, the problems, the electric atmosphere just before a deadline. Mistakes in copy can happen anywhere along the line in spite of careful checking. Food advertisements pose a special problem because prices fluctuate so rapidly. For example, when a food store manager corrects the proofs of his advertisement and sends them back, he is likely to change the prices on the ad. If his release with the corrections on it is misplaced in the composing room, then the advertisement goes to press without being corrected, and of course the advertiser is angry that his price is quoted incorrectly.

Sometimes mistakes are more embarrassing. Once a menswear store ran a two part advertisement. One was for jockey shorts and the other was for a game involving steel balls suspended from thin wires embedded in a wooden frame. When one ball is tapped it hits the next one and so on down the line—an expensive executive toy. The two advertisements were proofread and when a mistake was found, part of the type was reset. When the block of type was replaced, it was put into the right space but on the wrong page, so the ad for the underwear contained a phrase about balls bouncing in jockey shorts. Needless to say, the advertiser was upset.

Typographical errors occur in news stories in spite of careful proofreading. Sometimes proofreaders simply miss errors. Other times a line of type is reversed or a slug of type is inserted upside down or a printer's warm-up lines (which may be one letter typed over and over) slip into the paper.

Production problems can cause headaches too. The typed copy from the newsroom is transported downstairs to the composing room in a pneumatic tube. If a piece of copy gets stuck in the tube then more stories will back up behind it before the problem is discovered.

This kind of delay comes at a time when it is crucial to have copy moving to the printers at a regular pace. Sometimes it takes an hour or more to unblock the tube. A tray of type can be knocked over in the composing room and all the stories which had been placed in a certain order then have to be painstakingly reorganized or else reset completely.

In the pressroom all kinds of problems occur too. If a web from the rolls of paper breaks, the presses have to be stopped and the web reinserted. Or there can be an electrical failure, or the ink can become clogged, or a plate may fly off the press and smash up the press unit. All these problems require the presses to shut down until the problem is solved. And repairs have to be made quickly. The product is perishable: if the paper isn't on the street in the morning, it's too late.

Changes are taking place rapidly in newspaper production. The composing room of 1980 will be a very different place from the composing room of 1974. Instead of the noise and the printers running back and forth and the clattering of linotype machines, there will be a bank of computers in a silent room with computer operators sitting before them pushing buttons and looking into video screens.

Linotype was a technological innovation of the late 19th century which replaced the slow process of setting type by hand, letter by letter. Now computerized typesetters are replacing linotype; already the *Post* has converted from linotype to computerized typesetting for advertising. Within a few years the *Post* has gone from a manually operated typesetter, which produced lines of copy on photographic paper, to a machine which can set 200 lines a minute, to a machine which can set 400 lines a minute, to a machine which can set 1700 lines a minute.

These changes are of course very threatening to the linotype operators who see their jobs disappearing. Their fears have caused strikes, slowdowns, and long negotiations between the *Post*'s management and officials of the printers' union, the International Typographical Union. All the printers who now work for the *Post* are guaranteed jobs until they retire and substantial bonuses if they retire early, but no new printers are being hired. New skills will be required for setting type in the future.

The jobs of photoengravers are not threatened in the immediate future. Their skills are still required for making plates to reproduce photographs and advertising art work. Eventually their jobs will be eliminated because the images will be transferred to plastic plates by computer. The stereotypers who make the plates that go onto the presses will not be needed in a few years because the computerized typesetters will set type directly onto plastic plates. The pressmen who operate the press and the mailers who prepare the paper for delivery will be assured of jobs in the foreseeable future, as long as the end product is a newspaper which requires putting ink against paper and delivering the finished item to the public.

Like the reporters, advertising staff, secretaries, and telephone operators, the production people are members of unions, but these craft unions have somewhat different procedures than the American Newspaper Guild.

To start out in a craft union job a person must enter the trade as an apprentice, that is, a trainee. In Washington prospective apprentices apply for jobs through the newspaper publishers' association and an applicant takes the first opening available, either at the *Post* or the *Star-News*. In some of the unions, such as the printers' union and the stereotypers' union, no apprentices are being taken because no new jobs are opening up. In other towns, arrangements are different. Sometimes an applicant for an apprenticeship program goes directly to the union to apply and sometimes to the prospective employer. Some newspapers have non-union shops and in these cases a new employee is hired and trained directly by the newspaper and does not join a union at all.

Ronald Sweeney became an apprentice printer at the *Post* in 1966. He was interested in the newspaper business because his father worked in the circulation department at the *Washington Daily News.** He took an academic course in high school, thinking he would like to go to college and be a sportswriter.

When he realized that he wouldn't be able to go to college, he began aiming toward the printing trade, and while waiting for an opening at the *Daily News* he was offered an apprenticeship at the *Post*, which he took. Sweeney served a five-year apprenticeship as a printer, which was shortened by a year because he kept up with work that was assigned as part of the training program.

After his apprenticeship he was assigned to the night shift as a printer because, as he puts it, "I was low man on the priority board." After six weeks he managed to get back onto the day shift and he has been working on the day side ever since. Working days is what he likes but he has days off during the week and has to work weekends. This is a problem for Sweeney since his two school-age daughters would like their father to be at home on weekends and his wife feels that she is losing

* The *Washington Daily News*, an afternoon tabloid, was bought by the *Evening Star* in 1972. After the merger the *Star* became the *Star-News*.

out on social life with their friends who work Monday through Friday and have Saturdays and Sundays free.

Sweeney finished his apprenticeship when he was 22 years old and after about a year on the job he decided he didn't want to be just a printer for the rest of his life. So he went back to college at night and applied to be a supervisor. First he was a part-time supervisor, filling in for someone who was sick or on vacation and then he was made assistant supervisor. Now he is a supervisor and he hopes to go on and become a foreman and then production manager.

In his job as supervisor Sweeney moves around from day to day, doing various jobs. On Sundays and Mondays he is in charge of the computers in the composing room, making sure that they are set up properly and that material flows to them as it should. On Tuesdays he works in the paste-up department where advertisements are pasted onto grid sheets in the proper size and format so that metal plates can be made for the paper. And on Fridays he is in charge of keeping things moving in the area where all the news stories are run off for the paper.

This system of moving people around gives everyone a chance to learn how to manage a variety of different areas, and means that if somebody is absent from work another person can step into his slot and carry on. For Sweeney, who would like to move up to a management position, it is useful to be learning how all the different departments operate and fit together.

As a young apprentice, Sweeney used to go out and drink after work with the other printers, especially when he was on the night shift, but when he was made a supervisor he found that his relationships with the men changed somewhat. He had to give up some of the easy camaraderie without going so far as to be considered a snob because he had been made supervisor. He found that he had difficulty in some relationships at first but now he gets along well with most of the men.

As far as the changing technology is concerned, Sweeney finds himself in a very favorable position. The *Post* was changing over to computer operations when he was serving his apprenticeship so he was trained in the new processes. Many of the older printers are resistant to learning how to operate the new machines but Sweeney is enthusiastic about the new systems and is eager to learn how to operate the machines being introduced into the composing room.

For the most part Sweeney is very happy with the career he has chosen. He was lucky enough to become an apprentice printer at a time when he could get in on the ground floor and learn on the new machines as they were being introduced into the printing process. If he had applied for an apprenticeship a few years later, he would have found that there were no openings for apprentices.

He is pleased with the benefits, the pay, the vacations, and the working conditions. The work is clean; it does not involve physical labor or being outdoors in bad weather, and, for Sweeney, what is satisfying is that it is mentally challenging and it pays well. In 1974 printers were earning about $300 a week, which comes to nearly $16,000 a year.

When Sweeney's wife complains about how depressed she is that they can never go anywhere on weekends and tells him she wishes he had never become a printer, he reminds her of the money he is earning, his job security, medical benefits and pension plan. When she thinks it over, she has to agree with him that they are better off than many of their friends.

Bob Moe became production advertising manager

after various jobs in sales and advertising. For ten years he was an advertising salesperson at the *Post* and before that he sold life insurance and memberships in the American Automobile Association. Now part of his job is to maintain a liaison with the advertising agencies which submit ads and with the advertising department. His years in that department help him to understand the problems which can come up in the various stages of production.

Moe's day at the *Post* begins between seven-thirty and eight o'clock in the morning when he comes in to check on the ads which have been set during the night by the workers on the lobster shift. Most of his time is spent trouble shooting or dealing with problems.

An advertising salesperson comes in and complains that a client's ad is scheduled to run on March 31 when it should be run on March 3. Somebody wrote the number down wrong. So Moe has to look for the ad, find it somewhere in the composing room, and see if space can be found to dummy it onto the page where the advertiser wants it. A real estate broker who paid for a classified ad to run for a week complains that the ad was left out of this morning's paper. Moe has to trace down the ad, find out why it was omitted, and arrange for it to run for an additional day.

His job is hectic because the production process involves so many steps and so many people and so many places where things can go wrong. Simply tracing an error to its source can take him the better part of a day. "It all puts a few extra grey hairs in my head," he says.

In addition to supervising the daily production process, Moe also has to handle the preprinted advertising which appears in the Sunday paper. Preprints are sections such as Potomac magazine, TV Channels and

Parade, all of which are printed outside the *Post*'s plant and are shipped in during the week. In addition to these regular preprints, a customer preprint may be sent in, a small tabloid section printed up by one advertiser. Moe has to make sure that all of these preprints arrive on time, that the mail room is alerted for their arrival, and that there are not too many on one particular Sunday.

The labor problems caused by changing technology sometimes disrupt the composing room and cause many production problems. When people are dissatisfied with their work situation, or when they are learning a new technique which they are not enthusiastic about, then errors occur more frequently. In addition, Moe finds that because working with computers is so impersonal, people don't take as much pride in their work as they did when the trade was more of a craft.

Moe became interested in newspaper production as a boy growing up in Florida. He had a paper route for a small daily paper and worked in the mailroom. After his years of experience selling AAA memberships and life insurance, he decided he wanted a selling job with more regular hours. With life insurance he found that he was often working evenings because his clients were busy in the daytime.

He was attracted to the *Post* because the salespeople were paid salaries, instead of commissions, and they worked regular hours, nine to five. As production advertising manager he is trouble shooting sometimes from seven o'clock in the morning until seven o'clock at night.

"Of course," he says, "this is part of what I consider doing a good job, being loyal to the company. I consider this particular newspaper a very good company to work for, even though we have many faults."

The press room is run by Beverly Pendergast, the top

foreman, a well-built man in his early forties, with black sta-combed hair and a Virginia drawl. In 1949 he began his career in the *Post* pressroom as a flyman, a pre-apprentice position. As a flyman he had to spot the plates as they came down from the stereotype department. He took each plate as it arrived and placed it in the proper position on the press so that the pages came out in the right order when the paper was printed. Flymen also had to wash up the press, clean the floor in the pressroom, and bundle up waste paper and dispose of it.

After working as a flyman for a short while he could see that there was not much chance of moving up at the *Post* for a long time. There was a four- to six-year waiting list for apprentice openings before he could even get into the four-year apprenticeship program. Pendergast didn't want to wait that long, so he moved to Florida and was accepted right away into an apprenticeship program at the *Daytona Beach News-Journal*. When he had served his four-year apprenticeship, he came back to the *Post* as a journeyman, moved up to assistant foreman in charge of one of the presses, and then to foreman, in charge of the whole pressroom.

As an apprentice, Pendergast learned how to fasten the plates onto the press, how to set the rollers at the proper tension so that the paper would flow through without breaking, and how to start a roll of paper through the press. In those days you had to control a two-ton roll of paper with a small handbrake to keep it from spinning out of control or from being held so tight that it would break off. Now the tension of the paper in the rollers is controlled automatically.

A lot of the jobs which Pendergast learned to do by hand are now automatically controlled. For example, the press rollers used to be oiled by hand. Men walked up and down the row of presses every half hour or so, squirting a shot of oil into each of the rollers. Now the rollers have sealed bearings and oilers are no longer necessary. The union contract specifies that there must be a certain number of oilers on each shift, however, and so the oilers continue to walk up and down the pressroom even though they have nothing to do.

The union contracts specify the number of workers on each shift for other jobs also. Pendergast is a member of the union but, being a foreman, he tends to be sympathetic toward the management point of view. He once visited a non-union pressroom and saw that there were one-third the number of workers on each shift as there are at the *Post*.

He thinks both of cost and morale problems. It is, of course, expensive to keep workers on a shift when it isn't really necessary, and he finds that people are bored when there isn't anything to do but walk up and down the presses checking minor details during a seven- or eight-hour shift.

Pendergast expects to see much more automation and computer technology in the pressroom in the next ten or fifteen years and he is learning as much about it as he can through training programs and by reading trade journals. "If you just set here and let all this stuff come along, there'll be somebody else in here working on it," he says.

Since he has been at the *Post* he has seen the speed of the press go from 36,000 papers an hour to 72,000 papers an hour, and it is likely that in the future, the rate of speed will be increased by a substantial percent. A few years ago when a roll of paper ended, the presses had to be stopped while a new roll was pasted on by hand. Now the rolls can be spliced automatically while the press is running at full speed. Within the next fifteen years he can see that printing will probably be computerized to the point where plates will not be necessary. Pages will be made up in the composing room by computer and by pushing a button the makeup editor will be able to transfer the image directly to the press. Such a system will cut down on the need for workers trained as pressmen under the present system. But Pendergast observes, "You still have to feed paper to it and if guys are going to keep up with this technology there's going to be a tremendous amount of maintenance on it, I imagine."

Working conditions are changing in the pressroom too. Pressmen are supposed to wear surgical masks and ear protectors when they are working to keep from breathing in dust and ink mist and to protect their hearing from the noise of the press.

Under the terms of a federal law, the Occupational Safety Hazards Act, the noise, dust, and mist levels have to be cut down and the *Post* is experimenting with various ways of complying with the law—changing the ink, blowing the dust out of the room, and so on. So far Pendergast has not found any of these methods satisfactory and thinks that the best system will be to enclose the presses and keep the controls on the outside so that the sound will be deadened and the dust and mist contained within the enclosure.

He has gotten used to noisy working conditions, though perhaps he has lost some of his hearing through exposure to noise over a long period of time. "My wife tells me I'm deaf all the time," he says, "but I tell her I think I just turn off."

He also got used to working at night for many years. Since the presses run from about ten-fifteen at night until four-thirty in the morning, the night shift is the time when there is the most action for a pressman. Pendergast was on the night shift for twenty years and he liked it. There was no traffic on the streets when he was going home or coming to work. He slept in the morning, worked around the house in the afternoon, and was with his two sons when they came home from school.

As general foreman he is on the day shift, dealing with maintenance, ordering supplies, and handling grievances. He comes in at night once or twice a week to see how the presses are running, but the day and night foremen can handle this work for the most part. It took Pendergast nearly six months to get used to going to bed before midnight and getting up early enough to be at work by nine o'clock in the morning.

Pendergast reads the *Post* regularly. ("Best paper around," he says.) But as a pressman he has a specialized eye. A typesetter looks for typographical errors; a reporter for content and style; a makeup editor for page layout. A pressman looks for flaws in the printing, a faded page, or a color that hasn't turned out just right. "A lot of people look at it and say it really looks good but to me it could look terrible," he says.

He has few complaints about choosing a career as a pressman. "It's been good for me and for most guys working in it. But you see some kids come in and they just don't like it," he says. The noise and dust turn a lot of people off, but, as he points out, these conditions are being changed. The money is good. A pressman can earn up to $30,000 a year with overtime. Since it is a field where changes are taking place rapidly, the main requirements would be a background in computer technology, and an ability to learn and to adapt to new situations.

CHAPTER 18

Delivering the Newspaper

The distribution of the *Post* is handled by a network of independent dealers and carriers working under the supervision of the *Post*'s circulation department. Unlike the advertising department where there are no commissions and no direct rewards for selling, the circulation department operates on an incentive system. The dealer's earnings are dependent on the number of papers he sells to the carrier, and the carrier's earnings depend on how many customers he has. Many newspapers operate differently with distribution handled by employees of the paper, salaried and unionized, and only the carriers who deliver the paper door to door being independent business people.

John Fuog is one of the *Post*'s 279 full-time dealers and John Finnegan is one of the 6000 carriers. Fuog is a young man in his twenties and Finnegan is a high school sophomore. Fuog distributes about 3400 newspapers a day to 40 carriers in the Fairfax County, Virginia, suburbs. John Finnegan, one of the 40 carriers, delivers 200 papers a day, mostly in three-story apartment buildings, including the one where he lives.

The two Johns are sitting in Fuog's office on a Saturday morning after they have made their deliveries. The office, which Fuog shares with six other dealers, is a two room suite, filled with wooden desks. It's a part of the suburban scene, in a small shopping center, next to a 7-11 store and a dry cleaners. The phone rings occasionally and other dealers come in and out.

Sitting with Fuog and Finnegan is Paul Poff, a small, dark man with a quiet voice, who is one of the *Post*'s assistant home delivery managers. He keeps in touch with the dealers who are assigned to him, finds out whether they are having problems, helps them deliver their papers if there has been a late press run and they are behind schedule, delivers a route if a carrier has failed to come up with a substitute, and trains new dealers. Poff was a dealer himself for nine years and his children have a *Post* route which he and his wife help them with.

John Fuog is a cheerful man who speaks enthusiastically about his job. He has been a dealer for about a year and before that learned his way around by working for other dealers on their day off.

His day begins around one-thirty a.m. when he drives his van from Virginia to the *Post* building in downtown Washington to pick up his papers. He goes into a driveway at the side of the building and pulls his truck up to one of the loading docks in a row along the wall. He has a special key which he inserts into a lock. Each dealer's key is coded by computer to his number and when the key is turned in the lock, the computer sets up his load with the proper number of newspapers to come down the chute where he is waiting for them. The locked door opens and the papers start moving along a conveyor belt which reaches to within three feet of the open door of the truck. Fuog loads in his papers and by two-thirty he should be ready to leave, unless there has been a late press run, a labor slowdown, bad weather, or some other problem.

The papers are tied with baling wire into bundles containing varying numbers of newspapers depending on the size. If the papers are very large, 92 to 112 pages, each bundle holds 25 papers. When the newspaper is lighter there are more papers per bundle.

After picking up all the papers, Fuog drives back to Virginia and leaves the papers at preassigned drop points where the various carriers pick them up. Sometimes he also has to deliver a route or two himself if he is short of carriers. Then he goes back to his office to do his paper work, "detail work," he calls it, and wait for any complaints from customers, which might come to his office directly or through the circulation department at the *Post*. When he leaves his office around nine a.m., he is ready for a few hours sleep.

John Fuog does not find his life at all restricted by his night hours. In fact, he would rather work at night than in the daytime because he can plan his sleeping hours according to what he wants to do. If he has an evening engagement, he can sleep all day. If he has something to do in the morning, he can sleep in the afternoon and evening, or he can sleep on split shifts in the morning and evening if he wants to do something in the afternoon. Fuog is not married so he does not have the problem of coordinating his schedule with those of a wife and children.

(Paul Poff recalled that when he was a dealer, his children didn't even think he worked because they only saw him when he was sleeping or relaxing.)

Fuog has hired a man to work for him on Saturday and Sunday so that he can have the weekends off. In its contracts with dealers, the *Post* agrees to provide them with a gross sum which they can use to hire a driver so that they can take time off and to pay for insurance, gasoline, oil, depreciation on their trucks and other expenses. Each dealer negotiates his contract individually with the home delivery manager and his particular situation determines his gross—how many miles he has to travel, whether he has office and telephone expenses, any condition which raises his expenses.

Normally, a dealer has to make a large outlay to get started in his dealership. He has to purchase a truck and he has to be bonded. Fuog was lucky because he was able to buy a truck from another dealer and pay for it on an installment plan, and a friend lent him the money which he was required to put up for the bond. He was bonded for $25,000, of which he had to put up ten percent when he took the dealership, and pay an additional ten percent over twenty months. The *Post* protects itself by requiring the dealers to be bonded. If a dealer fails to fulfill his contract or disappears without paying for his newspapers, the *Post* can collect the money he owes from the bonding company which has issued the bond.

Many dealers find that they form close relationships with the carriers who work for them. John Finnegan has worked for four dealers and he has had the best relationships with John Fuog and his predecessor who take the time to talk to him and his parents when they bring in their bill each month.

John Finnegan has been delivering papers for about three years but has had a *Post* route for only about a year. He was very pleased when he got the opportunity to switch to a morning route because he did not like to have his afternoons after school completely taken up with work.

Now he gets up at four in the morning, begins delivering papers around four-thirty and is finished by about six-thirty. He has been delivering three routes but expects to give up one when Fuog finds another carrier. Fuog places the newspapers for him at two drop points so that he does not have to carry them for long distances and John Finnegan comes to the drop points with a cart, something like a shopping cart, especially designed for carrying newspapers.

Because he has an apartment route, he can deliver a large number of papers fairly fast, unlike a single family house route where it takes a long time to cover only a few customers. Many carriers prefer apartment routes because they can make more money from them but on the other hand it is usually harder to collect from apartment customers than from homeowners. There is a higher turnover of people and customers are often not at home when the carrier comes to collect every month. John Finnegan has solved this problem, however, by taking self-addressed envelopes to his customers and having them mail their payment to him.

On Sundays he pays a friend to deliver one of the three routes he serves. The 256 Sunday papers which he is responsible for weigh nearly half a ton and he could not deliver to all his customers on time. His friend also helps him out if he is sick or wants to go on vacation during the summer.

John expects to continue delivering newspapers until he goes to college. When he talks to his friends who have part-time jobs, he realizes that he is lucky to have a paper route. He works about two hours a day, seven days a week and once a month he has to spend a few hours keeping track of his accounts. He clears about $275 a month which means that he is earning over four dollars an hour. He doesn't know any other high school students who are earning more than that.

By about seven in the morning when John Finnegan is at home eating breakfast and John Fuog is in his office keeping track of his accounts, the circulation department at the *Post* is beginning to function. The people who work in the service department are sitting at telephone consoles with headsets over their ears taking complaints from customers who have not received their newspapers. The person taking the complaint then notifies the dealer or the dealer phones in before eight-thirty to collect any complaints and then delivers the papers.

After complaints come calls about stopping or starting delivery—people going on vacation or coming home, people starting new subscriptions, people cancelling subscriptions. All these notices are tabulated and at five o'clock each afternoon the circulation department sends the mailroom the number of newspapers which each dealer is to receive that day. Then the mailroom makes up the appropriate number of bundles and extra papers for each dealer.

From the top down the circulation department is run by Jack Patterson, vice president for circulation, and V. T. Curtis, circulation manager. Patterson is a brisk grey-haired man with an abrupt manner. He is a westerner who came to the *Post* after managing circulation on papers in Seattle, San Francisco, and Los Angeles. "Vee" Curtis is a native of Washington, D.C., who began his career in newspaper circulation as a carrier in his own neighborhood as a schoolboy. He worked for the *Times-Herald* until 1954 when the *Post* bought it and he has been with the *Post* ever since.

Patterson and Curtis each have a large office with a window, decorated with the *Post*'s standard modern furniture. Curtis, a stocky, grey-haired man with stained teeth, leans back in his swivel chair and chews on a fat cigar. The shelf behind his desk is filled with thick notebooks containing circulation figures for the *Post* and the *Star-News* and all kinds of information about carriers—equipment, contests, scholarships, and promotions.

According to the circulation department's organizational chart Patterson is in charge of the entire department and the director of overall planning, while Curtis is his administrative assistant and second in charge of the department. He oversees all the promotion connected with dealers and carriers.

Patterson holds a meeting every Monday morning with the home delivery managers and other supervisory personnel to report any changes in policy or procedure which may affect dealers and carriers and to hear reports from the field staff on any problems or successes which they have.

He is concerned with overall and county circulation figures— how this year's sales compare with last year's and how the *Post*'s sales compare with the *Star-News*'s. In areas where the *Post* is behind the *Star-News* or where the *Star-News* has made gains, he is particularly looking for ways to increase sales.

According to 1974 figures the *Post* surpasses the *Star-News* in all of metropolitan Washington except daily in Charles County, Maryland, a predominantly rural area. The *Post*'s total daily net paid circulation in the metropolitan area was 532,641 and the *Star-News*'s was 391,633, a 36% lead for the *Post*. The *Post*'s highest percentages of coverage were in the wealthy suburban counties, a fact which is, of course, of interest to advertisers.

Curtis is in charge of all promotions and incentives to encourage carriers to increase their sales. There is a catalog of prizes which carriers can earn by increasing the circulation on their routes. They get four points for every daily and Sunday subscription, three points for a daily only subscription and one point for a Sunday only subscription. These can be applied to a hundred or more prizes designed to appeal to teenage boys and girls—bicycles, camping equipment, record players, desk lamps, clothes.

In addition to the prizes, there are free trips for carriers, some of which are chosen by lot and others by judge. The *Post* sponsors free trips to Disney World and co-sponsors with Parade, a nationwide Sunday magazine supplement, a spring vacation trip to a different country every year. The three or four *Post* carriers to go are selected by a panel of judges and are chosen on the basis of their school activities, their outside activities, and their paper route activities.

There are a host of other shorter trips as well to nearby places of historical interest such as Gettysburg, Pennsylvania, and Williamsburg, Virginia, and to ski areas in the mountains of Pennsylvania or West Virginia. Paul Poff once volunteered to chaperone a ski trip, above and beyond his responsibilities as assistant home delivery manager, and enjoyed the experience so much that he has taken up skiing himself.

John Finnegan, who is a conscientious carrier, has never become interested in the prizes, the contests, and the trips. He finds that with school and sports activities and social life he does not have time to make a lot of effort to recruit new customers. Since he has an apartment house route, it is also difficult for him to see when people are moving in and out. The building managers are not cooperative in giving him forwarding addresses when people move, much less in telling him when someone has moved in. So he just does his job and does not strive to be a super salesperson.

A newspaper's success is measured by its circulation and its advertising revenue. Needless to say, the two go hand in hand. When circulation is high, advertisers are encouraged to buy advertising space because they know that they will be reaching a large audience. Conversely, a wide range of retail and classified advertising provides an incentive for people to buy the newspaper and increases circulation.

Ever since 1954 when the *Post* purchased the *Times-Herald* and absorbed its larger circulation, advertising and circulation revenue have been increasing. Circulation accounts for only fifteen percent of the *Post*'s revenue; the rest comes from advertising. Without high circulation, however, advertising revenue would drop. This is why Vee Curtis is thinking up new gimmicks to provide incentives for carriers to sell more newspapers.

CHAPTER 19

The Future

Money is very much on the minds of people at the *Post* these days. Members of the Newspaper Guild recently went on strike and, after the strike was settled, the top reporter's minimum wage was $423.25. In 1975 it becomes $448.25, plus a cost-of-living adjustment; the cost of newsprint has risen from $200 a ton to $260 a ton in a little over a year.

Cost problems like these are demanding hard thinking of the *Post*'s managerial staff. Since the cost of newsprint has risen $60 per ton in a year and the *Post* uses 400 tons a day, that means a cost increase of $24,000 a day. And since the price of ink has gone from six cents a pound to twelve cents a pound and the *Post* uses between 8000 to 15,000 pounds per day (depending on the size of the paper), the cost increase runs from $480 to $900 a day.

Paper and labor being the major expenses, economies in these areas are being considered. Even more important, thought is being given to the content of the paper. What will go on those pages of expensive newsprint?

The *Post* is not planning any immediate cost-cutting measures to conserve paper but undoubtedly in the future some will have to be taken. The cost of each newspaper will rise, probably to 25 cents, and then the question becomes, will a price increase permanently decrease circulation? Some economies have already been made in the use of advertising; for example, the *Post* no longer prints large sections of advertising with one news story at the top of each page. This was a waste of news space, since, obviously, no important news reached these pages.

Some papers are cutting down on the number of comics they carry or reducing the size of each comic strip. Some are raising their advertising rates to force advertisers to take smaller ads at a higher cost. Others are reducing the size of their news hole—the amount of space devoted to news, but the *Post* would be reluctant to take this step.

To reduce labor costs, the *Post* is moving into computerized technology, a step which will require a large initial investment in machines but will eventually reduce the number of people needed to produce the paper. When fully installed, the new technological devices will change the paper from the newsroom to the press room.

The first change in the newsroom will be in the way copy is prepared. Already electric typewriters are beginning to replace the old manual ones at some desks and some of these electric typewriters have a typeface which can be read by a machine called an optical character reader (OCR). The typed sheet is inserted into the OCR, which reads the characters and transcribes them into a computer language. Then another computer produces photocomposed copy. This process is much faster than the present system in which a reporter's copy is retyped, either by a linotype or tape perforator operator.

An even more automated alternative to the OCR machine is the VDT tube, which may appear in the *Post*'s newsroom by the 1980s. In this system a reporter types his copy which then appears on a video screen rather than on paper. The reporter can rewrite the story, read the corrected copy on the screen, and then release it to be stored by the computer until it is needed for editing and headline writing. When the editors are through with it, it is set in type by the computer.

Page layouts will also be done by computer. Eventually there will be a video screen in the makeup room on which a whole page can be called up and the makeup person can push buttons to try different combinations of news and ads until the page is suitably laid out. Then it will be released to be impressed onto a plastic plate which goes onto the press. Eventually the plate will be eliminated and a computer will transfer the complete page image directly onto the press. This process, called jet printing, may be perfected within the next fifteen years.

Of course, a computer failure would be disastrous. The system will have to be designed with a reserve computer, perhaps one shared with other newspapers, which could take over in an emergency.

With all the emphasis on changing the production process, the *Post* business executives do not foresee that the end product will be greatly changed. Ink will still be applied to paper to make a printed product, which will then have to be sorted, bundled, and delivered. Even farther into the future there is talk of a final product which would not be printed at all but which would be transmitted by cable onto a home TV screen. Such a development is so far in the future that no one at the *Post* is even considering it as more than a remote possibility at the present time.

The introduction of this technology will have profound effects on the people who have to deal with it. It is already threatening the jobs of the printers and the stereotypers, and it will eliminate the jobs of many other employees who do not keep up with new developments. On the other hand, it may cut long-term costs enough to keep the newspaper alive for many years and insure future jobs.

In addition, the technological innovations will change the working habits of the many reporters who like to use manual typewriters. Tom O'Toole, who pounds out his science copy with two fingers, is unhappy about the prospective changes. He thinks they will dehumanize the business. Reporters will have to learn to type out perfect copy or make corrections in the manner required for the computer. During the period of change, there will probably have to be typists to retype the copy of some reporters.

Staff members on the business side and in the newsroom are dealing with the problems of setting up the new systems and helping people adjust to them. Martie Zad, the former sports editor, is now a liaison person, working both with the manufacturers of computer systems and with editors and reporters.

He describes his job as "putting sense into the overall system to be sure that it does what we want it to do and doesn't work like a computerized billing system for a dentist or something." He confers with editors and reporters to see how the computers can be adapted to meet their needs. He also attends seminars and conferences to learn how the new equipment works and to try it out himself.

He was surprised to find that he felt comfortable working on a video tube after half a day of practice. "I could certainly work it as well as I work with a typewriter or pencil," he said, "in either composing a story or editing a story. I was quite amazed that it is that simple and that the machine doesn't have to run the man. The man can run the machine quite easily."

In addition, he will set up training programs at the *Post* to show editors and reporters how to operate the new machines and will try to dispel their fears and uncertainties. Already training programs are going on in the production departments where computers were first introduced about ten years ago.

Publisher Katharine Graham keeps track of production costs and the introduction of new machinery. She is also interested in what is being written in the *Washington Post* and what should be written. In the heady days of the post-Watergate period, while the *Post* is riding the crest of a wave of adulation, she is concerned about the harmful effects of Watergate on the press and what the concerns of journalists should be in the future.

In a recent speech to the Magazine Publishers Association she pointed out some of the pitfalls facing the press as a result of its role in exposing the Watergate crimes, and she indicated directions in which she thought it should be going.

First of all, she said, "The manner in which the stories of corruption and misuse of power unfolded made the press too much . . . an actor in the drama which was being played out. Some individuals became celebrities, and the whole profession became regarded as heroic. That is an unnatural role, and to some extent a dangerous one, which was thrust on us by . . . the default of the other institutions, such as the opposition party and the agencies of justice."

. She points out that the experience of reporting the Watergate story made reporters excessively mistrustful of public officials because they were deceived over and over again. As a result, the press is now zealously investigating the finances of public officials and interrogating government spokesmen, on the assumption that they have something to hide.

Katharine Graham finds the reaction of reporters and editors understandable. But she warns against being trapped by the experience of Watergate and limited to asking the same kinds of questions to uncover the major stories of the late 1970s. Watergate, she points out, was rather simple compared to the stories that the press has to deal with now. Watergate was a conspiracy which required traditional investigative techniques to uncover and which revolved around a few actors.

The new stories are much more complicated. The issues of oil, food shortages, and environmental pollution do not lend themselves neatly to crisis coverage or to traditional investigative techniques.

The reporters who cover these stories, says Mrs. Graham, will have to be able "to comprehend a number of extremely arcane fields, ranging from macroeconomics to geology to antitrust." Understanding a field in which one is not a specialist is difficult in the best of circumstances and is made even harder by experts working to keep their field obscure.

Katharine Graham does not expect the press to win any popularity contests in the future. "Those of us in the news business," she says, "might as well reconcile ourselves to the fact that we probably face some more years of delivering exceedingly bad news." The press will continue to be accused of reporting what's wrong, of tearing down institutions and undermining public confidence.

The answer to these accusations, she says, is that the press does not tear down; nor does it build up. "Our job is to relate what's happening, as fairly and completely as we can—whether or not that is what people want to hear and what officials want the people to believe."

The business of the press is information, and, Katharine Graham says, "the democratic system . . . is grounded on the premise that the people should be informed, that, indeed, they can make intelligent decisions only when they are fully informed."

She sums up her view of the role of the press in the

future by saying, "How we perform will . . . determine the extent to which the press remains healthy and strong and, if not always well regarded, at least well read."

The future of the *Post* will depend on sound business management and wise moral leadership. Katharine Graham as a business executive is of course concerned about profits (and the *Post*'s profits are healthy) because without a strong, independent financial base a newspaper is not free to print what it sees fit or, for that matter, free to print anything at all. But as a journalist and a member of a family with a strong tradition of public service and civic responsibility, she also exercises the moral and professional leadership which is required to make the *Washington Post* not just a well-managed corporation but a solid national institution which fulfills its mandate to inform the public.

Index

216

218

The Washington Post

FINAL

132 Pages—5 Sections

Amusements	B 5	Real Estate
Classified	D 7	Comics
Editorials	A18	Financial
Fed. Diary	E49	Sports
Metro	D 1	Style
Obituaries	D 6	TV-Radio

The Weather

Today—Fair, high around 60, low in the 30s. Chance of precipitation in 10 per cent today and 40 per cent tonight. Sunday—Cloudy, high in the 50s. Temp. range: Today, 61-38; Yesterday, 54-33. Details on page D4.

97th Year · · · No. 108   © 1974, The Washington Post Co.   SATURDAY, MARCH 23, 1974   Phone (202) 223-6000   Classified 223-6200 / Circulation 223-6100

Budget Reform Advances

Senate-Passed Version Goes To Conference

By Spencer Rich
Washington Post Staff Writer

The Senate, intent on recapturing the constitutional power of the purse from the White House, yesterday approved a revolutionary congressional procedure of handling the government's $300 billion annual budget. The vote was 80 to 0.

The bill, which now goes to conference with a similar House measure, is a key element in the lawmakers' drive to reclaim decision-making powers that have passed to the White House through congressional sloth and disorganization.

It would create congressional budget committees to consider all federal spending each year as a whole, fix a target surplus or deficit, clamp a ceiling on total outlays, and divvy up the total among 14 broad categories, such as health and defense, and thus assign priorities.

For lack of such mechanism in its creaky procedures, sponsors said, Congress in practice has yielded real control over most budget decisions to the White House, which has a well-staffed, centralized Office of Management and Budget capable of coordinating all parts of the budget into a fiscal whole.

They said the new legislation, which also would create a congressional office of the budget (similar in scope to the General Accounting Office) to provide technical expertise, would give Congress the capability to make budget decisions on its own, rather than relying on the White House.

By June 1 and again in September, Congress is to pass resolutions setting out target spending figures for the government as a whole and for each of the 14 major program categories.

The Appropriations committee would continue to act on the spending bills, within the Budget committees' guidelines. If the total adopted in the September target resolution is exceeded by the total of the individual bills, a cutback to comply with the target would have to be enacted.

The bill also would forbid the President to impound or withhold for policy purposes any funds voted by Congress.

The drive to revive the powers of Congress over key elements of national life has already led to passage, over a veto, of legislation curbing the President's power to wage undeclared war unless Congress assents, and passage of a bill requiring Senate confirmation of the OMB director. Also part of the drive are efforts to enact curbs on presidential fund impoundments and on executive withholding of documents from Congress. The present bill is another major effort in the same direction.

See BUDGET, A8, Col. 3

Witness

Rose Mary Woods, President Nixon's secretary, is escorted by Capitol Police Inspector Leonard Ballard as she appears before the Watergate committee.

Associated Press

U.S. Air Force Is 'Stronger' Than Soviets', Chief Claims

By Michael Getler
Washington Post Staff Writer

Air Force Chief of Staff George S. Brown says that the service he heads "overall is a stronger . . . more proficient and professional force" than the Soviet air arm and that factor-acquaintance leadership is a big factor.

The four-star general's enthusiasm for the capabilities of its service comes at a time when military leaders in other branches, particularly the Navy, are painting grim comparisons between U.S. forces and their Soviet counterparts.

During a wide-ranging interview in his Pentagon office, the Air Force's top officer focused on measures other than hardware as a way to equate rival forces.

Without getting into the pros and cons of Vietnam, the general simply pointed out that "that war lasted a helluva long time."

One result, he said, is that "we don't have anyone in any echelon of command in a responsible position who isn't combat experienced. That

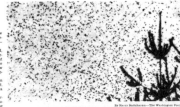

GEN. GEORGE S. BROWN
. . . 'more professional'

than those of the Soviet Union." In contrast to what Brown sees as a Soviet fighter force oriented to defense, he said "our tactical forces are trained and equipped to work offensively" in carrying the battle to an enemy.

The general's assessment of U.S. Air Force superiority extends into the airlift and bomber fields as well.

The Soviets, as is well known, "have no bomber force comparable" to the large 496-plane U.S. fleet of long-range B-52 and FB-111 strategic bombers.

The Russians do, however, have a very large bomber defense network of anti-aircraft guns, missiles and fighters. But, under questioning, Brown acknowledged that U.S. estimates indicate that 70 to 80 per cent of the American planes—assuming they are not destroyed on the ground in a surprise attack—could either get through or go around those defenses, attacking from various points around the huge Soviet land mass.

means a lot in terms of being used to the equipment, the tactics and the people. They've all been exposed to gunfire."

The Soviet Union has stayed out of combat since the end of World War II.

All things considered, the general stated, "our tactical forces are far more proficient

See BROWN, A7, Col. 1

EPA Asks Delay In Clean-Air Rules

By William Claiborne
Washington Post Staff Writer

The Nixon administration asked Congress yesterday to adding "flexibility" to current environmental standards of air pollution control in heavily polluted cities, and to authorize the government to order electric utilities to shift from oil to coal burning furnaces.

The administration also proposed delaying for two years implementation of automobile antipollution standards, meaning that emission limits for 1975 model cars would be acceptable for 1976 and 1977 models.

The retreat from the original standards of the 1970 Clean Air Act is needed to balance the nation's environmental and energy needs, according to Russell E. Train, administrator of the Environmental Protection Agency.

Train, who unveiled a package of Clean Air Act amendments he sent to Con-

gress, defended the plan as a "realistic" approach to the air pollution dilemma. "But in response to question of he said some of the proposals would not have been his personal choice.

In fact, Train said, he could not accept two administration proposals, one of which would revoke the law's requirement that existing clean air not be allowed to deteriorate as low as current minimum protective standards and another that would permit power plants to use anti-pollution equipment when they exceed the air air pollution demands are not violated.

Train said he was sending those proposals to Congress as "issues" for debate, but not as legislative recommendations.

The measure was introduced by Sen. Robert Dole (R-Kan.) yesterday and

See POLLUTE, A12, Col. 1

D.C. to End Restriction On Gas Sale

By LaBarbara Bowman and Paul Hodge
Washington Post Staff Writers

D.C. Mayor Walter E. Washington said yesterday the city's voluntary odd-even plan for gas purchases end next Friday.

"We are returning to normalcy," the mayor said ing a news conference, "so we're taking the wraps o

The mayor instituted the voluntary system, which c nated in Oregon, on Feb. 11, almost simultaneously with Maryland and Virginia jurisdictions. It is an attempt to end the lengthening gas lines which had soaked around every open service station, as motorists reacted to the gas shortage.

The odd-even plans in Maryland and Virginia will continue for the immediate future.

Although the odd-even plan is being suspended in Washington on Friday, the mayor said he was still encouraging gas stations to serve only cars which need at least one-half tank of gas.

In other energy announcements the mayor added:
• Eight gas stations throughout the city will be open from day from 10 a.m. to 6 p.m. because of having gasoline allotted to them by the city. The mayor instituted the Sunday opening last Sunday with four stations.
• The number of stations remaining open from 7 to 9 p.m. also made possible by allocations from the city, will be reduced from 20 to 12 because business has fallen off, making some of them unnecessary.

Some stations have started staying open later without special allocations of city gas.

The city's increased gas allocation for March of 19.3 million gallons, compared to 18.3 million in February, has made the odd-even plan unnecessary, the mayor said. "The long lines have disappeared and the situation is almost back to normal," he added.

"The prospects for continued improvement appear favorable based on the premise of increased gasoline allocations stemming from the lifting of the oil embargo," the mayor said.

Although he forecast normal levels, Mayor Washington added that he still intends to ask Congress for legislation giving him the right to institute some mandatory controls if the gas situation worsens in the future.

Some of his aides have explained that these usually doubted.

See ALLOCATE, A8, Col. 3

U.S. Cuts Oil, Gas Estimate

By George C. Wilson
Washington Post Staff Writer

President Nixon's pressed hopes for Ameri independence in fuel ceived a setback yester when new U.S. Geolog Survey figures showed substantially less oil and under the sea than the ernment previously had e mated.

Secretary of the Inter Rogers C. B. Morton t Congress in January tha looked as though 200 billi barrels of oil and 850 t lion cubic feet of natu gas could be obtained drilling into seabeds off t United States.

But new government survey circulated yesterd said the offshore lode cou be as low as 80 billion b rels of oil and 400 trilli cubic feet of gas—or counting that already tak from the sea bottom.

Several major policy d cision, including Preside Nixon's order for a 10-fo increase in leasing of shore tracts to oil com nies, were made under t higher estimates.

Thus "environment groups who have oppose accelerated leasing of t Outer Continental Shelf grounds it is too hurr have been handed a n argument.

The new estimates contained in a report by Council on Environmer Quality on offshore oil o erations. The same repo which became available y terday, warns that oil a gas be spilled on beaches if S

See RESERVES, A11, Col

Ford Renews Warning to Europeans

By John Hefferman
Reuter

A new warning to the European allies on the issue of possible reductions of American troops on the continent came yesterday from Vice President Gerald R. Ford.

He cautioned that there could be a unilateral troop cut by the United States unless the allies cooperated in trying to find a mutual and balanced force reduction with the Soviet Union.

Ford's comments were made in an exclusive interview with Reuter and came in the wake of the disclosure by secretary of State Henry A. Kissinger that American, British and German experts conferred in Washington this week on East-West troop reductions.

Without giving any details, Kissinger cited the tripartite talks as assuring a press conference Thursday that allied consultations were going on despite strains in the alliance.

Kissinger is scheduled to travel to Moscow next week for talks with the Soviets. Subjects are expected to include the current status of the strategic arms limitation talks, East-West security arrangements and possible agreement on mutual and balanced reduction of forces in Europe. Kissinger's trip is to prepare the way for a scheduled visit to Moscow by President Nixon this summer.

Ford said he was opposed to any decrease in American troop strength in Europe—a position also stated by Mr. Nixon Tuesday night in Houston—unless it was part of a mutual and balanced force reduction agreement with the Soviet Union. But he noted

See FORD, A5, Col. 1

6% Fuel Surcharge On Air Fares Set

By Jack Egan
Washington Post Staff Writer

The Civil Aeronautics Board viewed by the board after six citing a "precipitous rise in months, when the CAB will re-jet fuel price per gallon," will examine fuel prices.

allow a 6 per cent increase in domestic plane fares starting April 16.

The surcharge will be re-

U.S. Resumes Soviet Credits

After Attorney General William B. Saxbe ruled that U.S. credits to the Soviet Union are legal, the Export-Import Bank approved $74.9 million in loans to the Soviet Union, Poland, Romania and Yugoslavia.

Details on Page A2

At the same time, the board approved a coast-to-coast discount fare filed by Trans World Airlines. It requires reservations and a $20 deposit 90 days before departure. Discounts from normal coach fare range from 16 to 37 per cent, depending on time of year and day of the week.

The so called "demand scheduling" fare — virtually the only remaining coast-to-coast discount fare — will be available on flights between major Eastern cities, including Washington, and Los Angeles and San Francisco beginning July 8. American Airlines and United Air Lines, which also

See FARES, A8, Col. 1

act curbs on presidential fuel impoundments and on executive withholding of documents from Congress. The present bill is another major effort in the same direction.

Senate Appropriations Committee Chairman John L. McClellan (D-Ark.) said he would vote for the bill "reluctantly" because of extreme doubts that in practice it would work as planned. He called it "so fraught with complexities, so cumbersome and cumbersome" that it might hinder rather than help the goal of clamping a lid on spending. However, the bill's sponsors were more optimistic.

"The bill will give Congress means to deal in an orderly and comprehensive fashion with our most important decisions.

See BUDGET, A8, Col. 3

Senate Favors Transport to Funeral

POW Kin May Get Travel Pay

By Ron Shaffer
Washington Post Staff Writer

The U.S. Senate quickly passed a bill yesterday that would authorize the Pentagon to pay travel expenses for relatives attending funerals of American prisoners of war and servicemen classified as missing in action whose bodies have been recovered in Southeast Asia.

The measure was introduced by Sen. Robert Dole (R-Kan.) yesterday and was passed by voice vote of the Senate without

the usual process of committee study and hearings. Dole said he was prompted to introduce the bill by a story in Friday's editions of The Washington Post.

The Post reported that Cecile Abbott of Sacramento, Calif., thought it "inequitable" that government would not travel expenses for hers, and her 12-year-old son to end the burial in Arlington Cemetery of her husband, Navy Capt. John Abbott, a POW who died in captivity and whose remains were re-

leased earlier this month by Hanoi. He requested that he be buried in Arlington.

She contrasted that with the money the government spent to transport relatives of 56 POWs released 14 months ago to reunions in stateside hospitals, and to the White House for a presidential reception.

Presidential press secretary Gerald L. Warren said at the White House briefing yesterday that President Nixon had asked the Defense Department to "seek avenues" to assist Mrs. Abbott, and the department said it would do so.

Sen. Dole said he would ask the House leadership to vote on the bill Monday. The House was not in session yesterday.

3 Found Guilty of Tax Fraud

Three principal officers of the Pomponio real estate empire were found guilty in Alexandria yesterday of filing false income tax returns.

Details on Page D1

12 Campaig Reform Bill Killed in M

By Karlyn Barker
Washington Post Staff Writer

ANNAPOLIS, March 22 Maryland House committ killed a dozen campaign refo bills today, effectively end any possibility this year legislation restricting campa contributions.

Instead of tightening el tion law, the House commit amended a measure of G Marvin Mancel to quadru the amount of money that c legally can donate to st political candidates.

Currently, contributors v give candidates a maximum $2,500 in the course of a political campaign. The amendment by the Hou Committee on Constitution and Administrative La would permit contributors give $10,000 in each el tion.

"Everybody thought the 500 limit was unrealistic nobody had the guts to do thing about it (before)," committee chairman, Charles J. Krysiak (D-Ba more City) said. "I think committee took a stand."

Reform bills, he said, sho be aimed "at the big guys p ting the big money, not little guys running for t House of Delegates."

The measures killed by t committee included bills th would have banned corpor contributions by regulat gun loans and placed lim on campaign spending by s election.

These bills and the meas by Mandel to place a $ limit on cash contributio were proposed here by t wake of political scandals.

See MARYLAND, A6, Col.

Maryland redistricted by court.

Huge Flock Roosts Anyhow

Sunset Salvo Greets Birds

By Bill Richards
Washington Post Staff Writer

GRACEHAM, Md., March 22 — For more than two hours tonight, men booed and blasted away with an arsenal of noisemakers in an effort to rid this tiny Frederick County community of millions of birds.

Victory in tonight's engagement between men and birds—most of them starlings, blackbirds and grackles — apparently went to neither side.

At dusk, when the first aerial firecrackers and propane gas explosions boomed

out over the countryside, birds by the thousands that were headed for Edger Ervick's 60-acre pine grove, where they have spent the nights since last fall, wheeled and circled in the air, as if confused.

For a half hour they would not land, but as the sky darkened, clouds of birds cascaded into the grove.

About 8:15 p.m., the noise-making ceased for the night and Dr. Kenneth L. Crawford, chief veterinarian for the Maryland State Health Department and coordinator of the antibird campaign,

met with newsmen. His view was that this initial engagement—if not the campaign—was won by the birds.

"We lost tonight," he said, "because of a lack of fire-power in certain areas, but the battle isn't over. We will be back again tomorrow and we know what our problems are."

"Some of our people ran out of ammunition," he said, "and our crew call was a flop."

An hour later, encountering a reporter in a restaurant here, Crawford said he

See BIRDS, A6, Col. 1

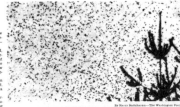

The birds of Graceham continue to swarm despite efforts to frighten them away.

By Harry Naltchayan—The Washington Post